HTML & CSS Concise Reference

HTML & CSS Concise Reference

Production Editor: Christopher Traynor

ISBN-10: 0-9818402-7-2
ISBN-13: 978-0-9818402-7-7

Published by Newport House Books
www.newporthousebooks.com

Newport
House

For all of the people that work tirelessly to make a difference in the lives of others…

Table of Contents

Introduction

HTML Tags

Appendixes

Index

Introduction

HTML (Hypertext Markup Language) was originally developed in the early 1990's by Tim Berners-Lee; the first implementation was in the Mosaic browser, developed at NCSA. Since then, it has seen explosive growth with the expansion of the web to the billions of pages it comprises today. During this time, HTML has been extended in a number of ways.

HTML 2.0 was developed under the guidance of the Internet Engineering Task Force (IETF) to embody those tags in common use as of late 1994. HTML+ and HTML 3.0, while never being officially adopted, proposed many significant language and feature enhancements. The World Wide Web Consortium's HTML Working Group produced yet another standard in 1997 - HTML 3.2 - that furthered the evolution of the language and brought us to the foundation for the current 4.0 standard covered in this reference.

With more than one browser vying for market share and the fact that a number of them have developed traction, browser-specific features and incompatibilities have been the result. Interoperability between browser versions is an important facet in the proliferation of the web, but sadly it does not seem to the be predominant design factor. This reference tries to remedy this by providing insights into the behavioral differences and support for all of the latest features of the language among the various browsers.

So, what is HTML exactly? It is, by design, a universal language for publishing interlinked documents. Put simply, it allows for the description of the layout of content in various media with the ability to specify the navigation between that content. Over time, various browsers have developed support for plug-ins that provide a means of extending the types of media that can be delivered through a web page. HTML serves as the foundation for that delivery in that it controls the rendering for the end user of a page. Within this language, there are facilities to allow for navigation, data entry in forms via various controls (eg. buttons, and text boxes) and visualization of data in text form, through tables and using graphics. Modern browser plug-ins provide the ability to view videos, play audio and interact in more dynamic ways than were envisioned by the original designer. This is where the power and ultimate longevity of HTML lies.

With HTML 4.0 there are now mechanisms such as style sheets, scripting, frames, embedding objects, improved support for right to left and mixed direction text, richer tables, and enhancements to forms, offering improved accessibility for people with disabilities. This reference covers these enhancements while providing full documentation on all of the features from previous versions of the language. Style sheets are covered in great detail as they compromise a giant leap forward in web page design. They can simplify HTML markup and largely relieve HTML of the responsibilities of presentation. They give both authors and users control over the presentation of documents - font information, alignment, colors, etc. The information for a given style can be specified for individual elements or groups of elements, making it easy to modify the look and feel of a portion or whole page by changing only a small section of the code. The style parameters for a page can be embedded directly or reside in an external file, making it possible to use them across a number of pages on a site.

How this book is organized

This HTML reference is divided into two parts: HTML elements and CSS properties. A decription is provided for each element or poperty along with the parameters, types, expected values, browser support, and related tags. While this is not a tutorial text, it can serve both the beginner and advanced web designer alike in providing the most up to date and complete reference on web page components. All elements and properties can be found in alphabetical order to make them easy to locate within the text. There are also a number of appendices containing further information that is not specific to a particular tag or property.

HTML Tags

<!--...-->

Description:
The comment tag is used to insert a comment in the source code. A comment will be ignored by the browser. You can use comments to explain your code, which can help you when you edit the source code at a later date. You can also store program-specific information inside comments. In this case they will not be visible for the user, but they are still available to the program. A good practice is to comment the text inside the script and style elements to prevent older browsers, that do not support scripting or styles, from showing it as plain text.

Requires closing tag:
No

Attributes:
None

<!DOCTYPE>

Description:
The `<!DOCTYPE>` statement is the very first thing in your document, before the `<html>` tag. This tag tells the browser which HTML or XHTML specification the document uses such as: `<!DOCTYPE HTML PUBLIC "-//W3C//DTD HTML 4.01 Transitional//EN">`

Requires closing tag:
No

Attributes:
None

<a>

Description:
The `A` element is used to define the source location of a hyperlink. The source anchor is used for the location of the instance and the web resource is the destination.

Requires closing tag:
Yes

Attributes:

NAME	VALUE	DESCRIPTION
accesskey	character	Optional. Allows the user to use keyboard keys for functions instead of a mouse.
charset	character_encoding	Optional. Specifies the character encoding of the content referred to by the link.
class	class_rule or style_rule	Optional. Assigns a class name or set of class names to an element.
coords	rect, circ, poly	Optional. This attribute specifies the position and shape on the screen.
dir	ltr or rtl	Optional. Sets the text direction to LTR (*Left To Right*) or RTL (*Right To Left*).
href	URL	Optional. Specifies the location of a Web resource, which defines a link between the source and the destination.
hreflang	language_code	Optional. Specifies the base language of the resource designated by `href` and may only be used when `href` is specified.
id	id_name	Optional. This attribute assigns a name to an element. This name must be unique within the

		document.
lang	language_code	Optional. Specifies the base language of an element's attribute for both values and text content.
name	section_name	Optional. This attribute names the current anchor so that it may be the destination of another link. *In future versions of XHTML the name attribute will be replaced by the id attribute!*
onclick	script	Optional. This event occurs when the user clicks on the user interface element.
ondblclick	script	Optional. This event occurs when the user double-clicks on the user interface element.
onkeydown	script	Optional. This event occurs when the user presses the specified key down on the user interface element.
onkeypress	script	Optional. This event occurs when the user presses and releases a key on the user interface element.
onkeyup	script	Optional. This event occurs when the user releases a key on the user interface element.
onmousedown	script	Optional. This event occurs when the user presses over the user interface element.
onmousemove	script	Optional. This event occurs when the user moves over the user interface element.
onmouseout	script	Optional. This event occurs when the user moves away from the user interface element.
onmouseover	script	Optional. This event occurs when the user moves over the user interface element.
onmouseup	script	Optional. This event occurs when the user releases the button over the user interface element.
rel	alternate, stylesheet, start,	Optional. Specifies the forward

	next, prev, contents, index, glossary, copyright, chapter, section, subsection, appendix, help, bookmark	link from the anchor specified by the `href` attribute to the current document.
rev	alternate, stylesheet, start, next, prev, contents, index, glossary, copyright, chapter, section, subsection, appendix, help, bookmark	Optional. This attribute is used to describe a reverse link from the anchor specified by the `href` attribute to the current document.
shape	rect, rectangle, circ, circle, poly, polygon	Optional. This attribute specifies the shape of a region and is used with the coords attribute.
style	style_definition	Optional. Specifies style information for the current element.
tabindex	number	Optional. Specifies the position of the current element in the tabbing order for the current document. The value must be a number between 0 and 32767.
target	_blank, _parent, _self, _top	Optional. This attribute specifies the name of the frame where the document is opened.
title	tooltip_text	Optional. Displays information about the specified element to which it is attached.
type	mime_type	Optional. Designates the MIME (*Multipurpose Internet Mail Extensions*) type of the target URL

<abbr>

Description:
The ABBR element allows authors to clearly indicate occurrences of abbreviations and acronyms. Western languages make extensive use of acronyms such as "GmbH", "NATO", and "F.B.I.", as well as abbreviations like "M.", "Inc.", "et al.", "etc.". Both Chinese and Japanese use analogous abbreviation mechanisms, wherein a long name is referred to subsequently with a subset of the Han characters from the original occurrence. Marking up these constructs provides useful information to user agents and tools such as spell checkers, speech synthesizers, translation systems and search-engine indexers.
The content of the ABBR element specifies the abbreviated expression itself, as it would normally appear in running text. The title attribute of these elements may be used to provide the full or expanded form of the expression.

Requires closing tag:
Yes

Attributes:

NAME	VALUE	DESCRIPTION
class	class_rule or style_rule	Optional. Assigns a class name or set of class names to an element.
dir	ltr or rtl	Optional. Sets the text direction to LTR (*Left To Right*) or RTL (*Right To Left*).
id	id_name	Optional. This attribute assigns a name to an element. This name must be unique within the document.
lang	language_code	Optional. Specifies the base language of an element's attribute for both values and text content.
onclick	script	Optional. This event occurs when the user clicks on the user interface element.
ondblclick	script	Optional. This event occurs when the user double-clicks on the user interface element.

onkeydown	script	Optional. This event occurs when the user presses the specified key down on the user interface element.
onkeypress	script	Optional. This event occurs when the user presses and releases a key on the user interface element.
onkeyup	script	Optional. This event occurs when the user releases a key on the user interface element.
onmousedown	script	Optional. This event occurs when the user presses over the user interface element.
onmousemove	script	Optional. This event occurs when the user moves over the user interface element.
onmouseout	script	Optional. This event occurs when the user moves away from the user interface element.
onmouseover	script	Optional. This event occurs when the user moves over the user interface element.
onmouseup	script	Optional. This event occurs when the user releases the button over the user interface element.
style	style_definition	Optional. Specifies style information for the current element.
title	tooltip_text	Optional. Displays information about the specified element to which it is attached.

See also:
`<ACRONYM>, <CITE>, <CODE>, <DFN>, <EM>, <KBD>, <SAMP>, <STRONG>, <VAR>`

<acronym>

Description:
The `ACRONYM` element allows authors to clearly indicate occurrences of abbreviations and acronyms. Western languages make extensive use of acronyms such as "GmbH", "NATO", and "F.B.I.", as well as abbreviations like "M.", "Inc.", "et al.", "etc.". Both Chinese and Japanese use analogous abbreviation mechanisms, wherein a long name is referred to subsequently with a subset of the Han characters from the original occurrence. Marking up these constructs provides useful information to user agents and tools such as spell checkers, speech synthesizers, translation systems and search-engine indexers.
The content of the `ACRONYM` element specifies the abbreviated expression itself, as it would normally appear in running text. The title attribute of this element may be used to provide the full or expanded form of the expression.

Requires closing tag:
Yes

Attributes:

NAME	VALUE	DESCRIPTION
class	class_rule or style_rule	Optional. Assigns a class name or set of class names to an element.
dir	ltr or rtl	Optional. Sets the text direction to LTR (*Left To Right*) or RTL (*Right To Left*).
id	id_name	Optional. This attribute assigns a name to an element. This name must be unique within the document.
lang	language_code	Optional. Specifies the base language of an element's attribute for both values and text content.
onclick	script	Optional. This event occurs when the user clicks on the user interface element.
ondblclick	script	Optional. This event occurs when the user double-clicks on the user interface element.

onkeydown	script	Optional. This event occurs when the user presses the specified key down on the user interface element.
onkeypress	script	Optional. This event occurs when the user presses and releases a key on the user interface element.
onkeyup	script	Optional. This event occurs when the user releases a key on the user interface element.
onmousedown	script	Optional. This event occurs when the user presses over the user interface element.
onmousemove	script	Optional. This event occurs when the user moves over the user interface element.
onmouseout	script	Optional. This event occurs when the user moves away from the user interface element.
onmouseover	script	Optional. This event occurs when the user moves over the user interface element.
onmouseup	script	Optional. This event occurs when the user releases the button over the user interface element.
style	style_definition	Optional. Specifies style information for the current element.
title	tooltip_text	Optional. Displays information about the specified element to which it is attached.

See also:
`<ABBR>, <CITE>, <CODE>, <DFN>, <EM>, <KBD>, <SAMP>, <STRONG>, <VAR>`

<address>

Description:
The `ADDRESS` tag defines all of the contact information for a document, section, company or the creator of the specified web page.

Requires closing tag:
Yes

Attributes:

NAME	VALUE	DESCRIPTION
class	class_rule or style_rule	Optional. Assigns a class name or set of class names to an element.
dir	ltr or rtl	Optional. Sets the text direction to LTR (*Left To Right*) or RTL (*Right To Left*).
id	id_name	Optional. This attribute assigns a name to an element. This name must be unique within the document.
lang	language_code	Optional. Specifies the base language of an element's attribute for both values and text content.
onclick	script	Optional. This event occurs when the user clicks on the user interface element.
ondblclick	script	Optional. This event occurs when the user double-clicks on the user interface element.
onkeydown	script	Optional. This event occurs when the user presses the specified key down on the user interface element.
onkeypress	script	Optional. This event occurs when the user presses and releases a key on the user

		interface element.
onkeyup	script	Optional. This event occurs when the user releases a key on the user interface element.
onmousedown	script	Optional. This event occurs when the user presses over the user interface element.
onmousemove	script	Optional. This event occurs when the user moves over the user interface element.
onmouseout	script	Optional. This event occurs when the user moves away from the user interface element.
onmouseover	script	Optional. This event occurs when the user moves over the user interface element.
onmouseup	script	Optional. This event occurs when the user releases the button over the user interface element.
style	style_definition	Optional. Specifies style information for the current element.
title	tooltip_text	Optional. Displays information about the specified element to which it is attached.

<applet>

Description:
Deprecated.

Requires closing tag:
Yes

Attributes:

NAME	VALUE	DESCRIPTION
align	left, right, top, bottom, middle, baseline, texttop, absmiddle, absbottom	**Deprecated. Optional. This attribute specifies the position of an IMG, OBJECT, or APPLET.**
alt	text	Optional. Specifies alternate text for user agents that cannot display images, forms, or applets.
archive	URL	Optional. Specifies a list of URI's to be preloaded that contain classes and other resources.
class	class_rule or style_rule	Optional. Assigns a class name or set of class names to an element.
code	URL	Optional. Specifies the class file name or the path to get the class file itself.
codebase	URL	Optional. Specifies the base URI for the applet. If it is not specified, then it defaults the same base URI as for the current document.
dir	ltr or rtl	Optional. Sets the text direction to LTR (*Left To Right*) or RTL (*Right To Left*).
height	pixels	Required. Specifies the initial height of the applet's display

		area.
hspace	pixels	**Deprecated.** Optional. This attribute specifies the amount of white space used to the left and right of an IMG, APPLET, or OBJECT.
id	id_name	Optional. This attribute assigns a name to an element. This name must be unique within the document.
lang	language_code	Optional. Specifies the base language of an element's attribute for both values and text content.
name	unique_name	Optional. Specifies a name for the applet instance, making it possible for applets on the same page to find each other.
object	Name	Optional. Names the resource of an applet's state interpreted relative to it's codebase.
onclick	script	Optional. This event occurs when the user clicks on the user interface element.
ondblclick	script	Optional. This event occurs when the user double-clicks on the user interface element.
onkeydown	script	Optional. This event occurs when the user presses the specified key down on the user interface element.
onkeypress	script	Optional. This event occurs when the user presses and releases a key on the user interface element.
onkeyup	script	Optional. This event occurs when the user releases a key on the user interface element.
onmousedown	script	Optional. This event occurs when the user presses over the user interface element.
onmousemove	script	Optional. This event occurs when the user moves over the user interface element.
onmouseout	script	Optional. This event occurs when the user moves away

		from the user interface element.
onmouseover	script	Optional. This event occurs when the user moves over the user interface element.
onmouseup	script	Optional. This event occurs when the user releases the button over the user interface element.
style	style_definition	Optional. Specifies style information for the current element.
title	text	Optional. Displays information about the specified element to which it is attached.
title	tooltip_text	Optional. Displays information about the specified element to which it is attached.
vspace	pixels	**Deprecated.** Optional. This attribute specifies the amount of white space used abve and below an IMG, APPLET, or OBJECT.
width	pixels	Required. Specifies the initial width of the applet's display area.

See also:
`<OBJECT>, <PARAM>`

Description:
The AREA tag specifies the shape of a hot spot in an image map allowing various shapes to be used as links.
Client-side Image Maps: When a user activates a region of a client-side image map with a mouse, the pixel coordinates are interpreted by the user agent. The user agent selects a link that was specified for the activated region and follows it.
Server-side Image Maps: When a user activates a region of a server-side image map with a mouse, the pixel coordinates of the click are sent to the server-side agent specified by the `href` attribute of the A element. The server-side agent interprets the coordinates and performs some action.

Requires closing tag:
Yes

Attributes:

NAME	VALUE	DESCRIPTION
accesskey	character	Optional. Allows the user to use keyboard keys for functions instead of a mouse.
alt	text	Required. For user agents that cannot display images, forms, or applets, this attribute specifies alternate text. The language of the alternate text is specified by the `lang` attribute.
class	class_rule or style_rule	Optional. Assigns a class name or set of class names to an element.
coords	rect, circ, poly	Optional. This attribute specifies the position and shape on the screen.
dir	ltr or rtl	Optional. Sets the text direction to LTR (*Left To Right*) or RTL (*Right To Left*).
href	URL	Optional. Specifies the location of a Web resource, which defines a link between the

		source and the destination.
id	id_name	Optional. This attribute assigns a name to an element. This name must be unique within the document.
lang	language_code	Optional. Specifies the base language of an element's attribute for both values and text content.
nohref	true, false	Optional. This attribute specifies that a region has no associated link.
onclick	script	Optional. This event occurs when the user clicks on the user interface element.
ondblclick	script	Optional. This event occurs when the user double-clicks on the user interface element.
onkeydown	script	Optional. This event occurs when the user presses the specified key down on the user interface element.
onkeypress	script	Optional. This event occurs when the user presses and releases a key on the user interface element.
onkeyup	script	Optional. This event occurs when the user releases a key on the user interface element.
onmousedown	script	Optional. This event occurs when the user presses over the user interface element.
onmousemove	script	Optional. This event occurs when the user moves over the user interface element.
onmouseout	script	Optional. This event occurs when the user moves away from the user interface element.
onmouseover	script	Optional. This event occurs when the user moves over the user interface element.
onmouseup	script	Optional. This event occurs when the user releases the button over the user interface element.
shape	rect, rectangle, circ, circle,	Optional. This attribute

	poly, polygon	specifies the shape of a region and is used with the coords attribute.
style	style_definition	Optional. Specifies style information for the current element.
tabindex	number	Optional. Specifies the position of the current element in the tabbing order for the current document. The value must be a number between 0 and 32767.
target	_blank, _parent, _self, _top	Optional. This attribute specifies the name of the frame where the document is opened.
title	tooltip_text	Optional. Displays information about the specified element to which it is attached.

<b>

Description:
Rendering of font style elements depends on the user agent. The following is an informative description only. It is possible to achieve a much richer variety of font effects using style sheets.

Requires closing tag:
Yes

Attributes:

NAME	VALUE	DESCRIPTION
class	class_rule or style_rule	Optional. Assigns a class name or set of class names to an element.
dir	ltr or rtl	Optional. Sets the text direction to LTR (*Left To Right*) or RTL (*Right To Left*).
id	id_name	Optional. This attribute assigns a name to an element. This name must be unique within the document.
lang	language_code	Optional. Specifies the base language of an element's attribute for both values and text content.
onclick	script	Optional. This event occurs when the user clicks on the user interface element.
ondblclick	script	Optional. This event occurs when the user double-clicks on the user interface element.
onkeydown	script	Optional. This event occurs when the user presses the specified key down on the user interface element.
onkeypress	script	Optional. This event occurs when the user presses and releases a key on the user

		interface element.
onkeyup	script	Optional. This event occurs when the user releases a key on the user interface element.
onmousedown	script	Optional. This event occurs when the user presses over the user interface element.
onmousemove	script	Optional. This event occurs when the user moves over the user interface element.
onmouseout	script	Optional. This event occurs when the user moves away from the user interface element.
onmouseover	script	Optional. This event occurs when the user moves over the user interface element.
onmouseup	script	Optional. This event occurs when the user releases the button over the user interface element.
style	style_definition	Optional. Specifies style information for the current element.
title	tooltip_text	Optional. Displays information about the specified element to which it is attached.

See also:
`<BIG>, <I>, <S>, <SMALL>, <STRIKE>, <TT>, <U>`

<base>

Description:
This attribute specifies an absolute URI that acts as the base URI for resolving relative URIs.

Requires closing tag:
No

Attributes:

NAME	VALUE	DESCRIPTION
href	URL	Required. Specifies the location of a Web resource, which defines a link between the source and the destination.
target	_blank, _parent, _self, _top	Optional. This attribute specifies the name of the frame where the document is opened.

<basefont>

Description:
The BASEFONT tag specifies font information for the entire document.

Requires closing tag:
No

Attributes:

NAME	VALUE	DESCRIPTION
class	class_rule or style_rule	Optional. Assigns a class name or set of class names to an element.
color	rgb(x,x,x), #xxxxxx, colorname	**Deprecated**. Optional. This attribute sets the text color.
dir	ltr or rtl	Optional. Sets the text direction to LTR (*Left To Right*) or RTL (*Right To Left*).
face	list_of_fontnames	**Deprecated.** Optional. Defines a list of font names the user agent should search for in order of preference.
id	id_name	Optional. This attribute assigns a name to an element. This name must be unique within the document.
lang	language_code	Optional. Specifies the base language of an element's attribute for both values and text content.
onclick	script	Optional. This event occurs when the user clicks on the user interface element.
ondblclick	script	Optional. This event occurs when the user double-clicks on the user interface element.
onkeydown	script	Optional. This event occurs when the user presses the

		specified key down on the user interface element.
onkeypress	script	Optional. This event occurs when the user presses and releases a key on the user interface element.
onkeyup	script	Optional. What to do when key is released
onmousedown	script	Optional. This event occurs when the user presses over the user interface element.
onmousemove	script	Optional. This event occurs when the user moves over the user interface element.
onmouseout	script	Optional. This event occurs when the user moves away from the user interface element.
onmouseover	script	Optional. This event occurs when the user moves over the user interface element.
onmouseup	script	Optional. This event occurs when the user releases the button over the user interface element.
size	default_text_size, (numbers are from 1 to 7)	**Deprecated.** Optional. This attribute sets the size of the font.
style	style_definition	Optional. Specifies style information for the current element.
title	tooltip_text	Optional. Displays information about the specified element to which it is attached.

See also:
`<FONT>`

<bdo>

Description:
The `bdo` (*Biodirectional Override*) element overrides the default text direction of `LTR` (*Left to Right*) text to `RTL` (*Right to Left*) placement.

Requires closing tag:
Yes

Attributes:

NAME	VALUE	DESCRIPTION
class	class_rule or style_rule	Optional. Assigns a class name or set of class names to an element.
dir	ltr, rtl	Optional. Sets the text direction to LTR (*Left To Right*) or RTL (*Right To Left*).
id	id_name	Optional. This attribute assigns a name to an element. This name must be unique within the document.
lang	language_code	Optional. Specifies the base language of an element's attribute for both values and text content.
style	style_definition	Optional. Specifies style information for the current element.
title	tooltip_text	Optional. Displays information about the specified element to which it is attached.

<big>

Description:
Rendering of font style elements depends on the user agent. The following is an informative description only. It is possible to achieve a much richer variety of font effects using style sheets.

Requires closing tag:
Yes

Attributes:

NAME	VALUE	DESCRIPTION
class	class_rule or style_rule	Optional. Assigns a class name or set of class names to an element.
dir	ltr or rtl	Optional. Sets the text direction to LTR (*Left To Right*) or RTL (*Right To Left*).
id	id_name	Optional. This attribute assigns a name to an element. This name must be unique within the document.
lang	language_code	Optional. Specifies the base language of an element's attribute for both values and text content.
onclick	script	Optional. This event occurs when the user clicks on the user interface element.
ondblclick	script	Optional. This event occurs when the user double-clicks on the user interface element.
onkeydown	script	Optional. This event occurs when the user presses the specified key down on the user interface element.
onkeypress	script	Optional. This event occurs when the user presses and releases a key on the user

		interface element.
onkeyup	script	Optional. This event occurs when the user releases a key on the user interface element.
onmousedown	script	Optional. This event occurs when the user presses over the user interface element.
onmousemove	script	Optional. This event occurs when the user moves over the user interface element.
onmouseout	script	Optional. This event occurs when the user moves away from the user interface element.
onmouseover	script	Optional. This event occurs when the user moves over the user interface element.
onmouseup	script	Optional. This event occurs when the user releases the button over the user interface element.
style	style_definition	Optional. Specifies style information for the current element.
title	tooltip_text	Optional. Displays information about the specified element to which it is attached.

See also:
`<B>, <I>, <S>, <SMALL>, <STRIKE>, <TT>, <U>,`

<blockquote>

Description:
The `blockquote` tag defines the start of a long quotation (block-level content).

Requires closing tag:
Yes

Attributes:

NAME	VALUE	DESCRIPTION
cite	URL	Optional. This attribute is intended to give information about the source from which the quotation was borrowed.
class	class_rule or style_rule	Optional. Assigns a class name or set of class names to an element.
dir	ltr or rtl	Optional. Sets the text direction to LTR (*Left To Right*) or RTL (*Right To Left*).
id	id_name	Optional. This attribute assigns a name to an element. This name must be unique within the document.
lang	language_code	Optional. Specifies the base language of an element's attribute for both values and text content.
onclick	script	Optional. This event occurs when the user clicks on the user interface element.
ondblclick	script	Optional. This event occurs when the user double-clicks on the user interface element.
onkeydown	script	Optional. This event occurs when the user presses the specified key down on the user interface element.

onkeypress	script	Optional. This event occurs when the user presses and releases a key on the user interface element.
onkeyup	script	Optional. This event occurs when the user releases a key on the user interface element.
onmousedown	script	Optional. This event occurs when the user presses over the user interface element.
onmousemove	script	Optional. This event occurs when the user moves over the user interface element.
onmouseout	script	Optional. This event occurs when the user moves away from the user interface element.
onmouseover	script	Optional. This event occurs when the user moves over the user interface element.
onmouseup	script	Optional. This event occurs when the user releases the button over the user interface element.
style	style_definition	Optional. Specifies style information for the current element.
title	tooltip_text	Optional. Displays information about the specified element to which it is attached.

See also:
<Q>

<body>

Description:
The `body` element defines the documents' body. It contains all the contents of the document (like text, images, colors, graphics, etc.).

Requires closing tag:
Yes

Attributes:

NAME	VALUE	DESCRIPTION
alink	rgb(x,x,x), #xxxxxx, colorname	**Deprecated.** Optional. Sets the color of hypertext links.
background	file_name	**Deprecated.** Optional. Designates an image generally tiled in the background of the specified page.
bgcolor	rgb(x,x,x), #xxxxxx, colorname	**Deprecated.** Optional. Sets the background color for the document body or table cells.
class	class_rule or style_rule	Optional. Assigns a class name or set of class names to an element.
dir	ltr or rtl	Opt Optional. Sets the text direction to LTR (*Left To Right*) or RTL (*Right To Left*).
id	id_name	Optional. This attribute assigns a name to an element. This name must be unique within the document.
lang	language_code	Optional. Specifies the base language of an element's attribute for both values and text content.
link	rgb(x,x,x), #xxxxxx, colorname	**Deprecated.** Optional. Sets the color of text marking unvisited hypertext links.
onclick	script	Optional. This event occurs

		when the user clicks on the user interface element.
ondblclick	script	Optional. This event occurs when the user double-clicks on the user interface element.
onkeydown	script	Optional. This event occurs when the user presses the specified key down on the user interface element.
onkeypress	script	Optional. This event occurs when the user presses and releases a key on the user interface element.
onkeyup	script	Optional. This event occurs when the user releases a key on the user interface element.
onmousedown	script	Optional. This event occurs when the user presses over the user interface element.
onmousemove	script	Optional. This event occurs when the user moves over the user interface element.
onmouseout	script	Optional. This event occurs when the user moves away from the user interface element.
onmouseover	script	Optional. This event occurs when the user moves over the user interface element.
onmouseup	script	Optional. This event occurs when the user releases the button over the user interface element.
style	style_definition	Optional. Specifies style information for the current element.
text	rgb(x,x,x), #xxxxxx, colorname	**Deprecated.** Optional. Sets the foreground color for text.
title	tooltip_text	Optional. Displays information about the specified element to which it is attached.
vlink	rgb(x,x,x), #xxxxxx, colorname	**Deprecated.** Optional. Sets the color of text marking visited hypertext links.

See also:

<HEAD>, <HTML>, <META>, <TITLE>

Description:
The `BR` element forcibly breaks (ends) the current line of text. For visual user agents, the `clear` attribute can be used to determine whether markup following the `BR` element flows around images and other objects floated to the left or right margin, or whether it starts after the bottom of such objects. To Prohibit a line break from occurring between two words: the   entity (or) acts as a space where user agents should not cause a line break.

Requires closing tag:
No

Attributes:

NAME	VALUE	DESCRIPTION
class	class_rule or style_rule	Optional. Assigns a class name or set of class names to an element.
id	id_name	Optional. This attribute assigns a name to an element. This name must be unique within the document.
style	style_definition	Optional. Specifies style information for the current element.
title	tooltip_text	Optional. Displays information about the specified element to which it is attached.

<button>

Description:
Buttons created with the BUTTON element function just like buttons created with the INPUT element, but they offer richer rendering possibilities: the BUTTON element may have content. For example, a BUTTON element that contains an image functions like and may resemble an INPUT element whose type is set to "image", but the BUTTON element type allows content.

Requires closing tag:
Yes

Attributes:

NAME	VALUE	DESCRIPTION
accesskey	character	Optional. Allows the user to use keyboard keys for functions instead of a mouse.
class	class_rule or style_rule	Optional. Assigns a class name or set of class names to an element.
dir	ltr or rtl	Optional. Sets the text direction to LTR (*Left To Right*) or RTL (*Right To Left*).
disabled	Disabled	Optional. Disables the control of user input.
id	id_name	Optional. This attribute assigns a name to an element. This name must be unique within the document.
lang	language_code	Optional. Specifies the base language of an element's attribute for both values and text content.
name	button_name	Optional. Specifies a unique name for the button
onclick	Script	Optional. This event occurs when the user clicks on the user interface element.
ondblclick	Script	Optional. This event occurs

		when the user double-clicks on the user interface element.
onkeydown	Script	Optional. This event occurs when the user presses the specified key down on the user interface element.
onkeypress	Script	Optional. This event occurs when the user presses and releases a key on the user interface element.
onkeyup	Script	Optional. This event occurs when the user releases a key on the user interface element.
onmousedown	script	Optional. This event occurs when the user presses over the user interface element.
onmousemove	script	Optional. This event occurs when the user moves over the user interface element.
onmouseout	script	Optional. This event occurs when the user moves away from the user interface element.
onmouseover	script	Optional. This event occurs when the user moves over the user interface element.
onmouseup	script	Optional. This event occurs when the user releases the button over the user interface element.
style	style_definition	Optional. Specifies style information for the current element.
tabindex	number	Optional. Specifies the position of the current element in the tabbing order for the current document. The value must be a number between 0 and 32767.
title	tooltip_text	Optional. Displays information about the specified element to which it is attached.
type	button, reset, submit	Optional. This attribute declares the type of the button.
value	some_value	Optional. This attribute assigns the initial value to the button.

See also:
<FORM>

<caption>

Description:
When present, the `CAPTION` element's text should describe the nature of the table. The `CAPTION` element is only permitted immediately after the `TABLE` start tag. A `TABLE` element may only contain one `CAPTION` element.

Requires closing tag:
Yes

Attributes:

NAME	VALUE	DESCRIPTION
align	left, right, top, bottom	**Deprecated.** Optional. Specifies the position of the caption with respect to the table.
class	class_rule or style_rule	Optional. Assigns a class name or set of class names to an element.
dir	ltr or rtl	Optional. Sets the text direction to LTR (*Left To Right*) or RTL (*Right To Left*).
id	id_name	Optional. This attribute assigns a name to an element. This name must be unique within the document.
lang	language_code	Optional. Specifies the base language of an element's attribute for both values and text content.
onclick	script	Optional. This event occurs when the user clicks on the user interface element.
ondblclick	script	Optional. This event occurs when the user double-clicks on the user interface element.
onkeydown	script	Optional. This event occurs when the user presses the

		specified key down on the user interface element.
onkeypress	script	Optional. This event occurs when the user presses and releases a key on the user interface element.
onkeyup	script	Optional. This event occurs when the user releases a key on the user interface element.
onmousedown	script	Optional. This event occurs when the user presses over the user interface element.
onmousemove	script	Optional. This event occurs when the user moves over the user interface element.
onmouseout	script	Optional. This event occurs when the user moves away from the user interface element.
onmouseover	script	Optional. This event occurs when the user moves over the user interface element.
onmouseup	script	Optional. This event occurs when the user releases the button over the user interface element.
style	style_definition	Optional. Specifies style information for the current element.
title	tooltip_text	Optional. Displays information about the specified element to which it is attached.

See also:
`<COL>, <COLGROUP>, <TABLE>, <TBODY>, <TD>, <TFOOT>, <TH>, <THEAD>, <TR>`

<center>

Description:
Centers enclosed text or embedded objects when enclosed between `CENTER` tags.

Requires closing tag:
Yes

Attributes:

NAME	VALUE	DESCRIPTION
class	class_rule or style_rule	Optional. Assigns a class name or set of class names to an element.
dir	ltr or rtl	Optional. Sets the text direction to LTR (*Left To Right*) or RTL (*Right To Left*).
id	id_name	Optional. This attribute assigns a name to an element. This name must be unique within the document.
lang	language_code	Optional. Specifies the base language of an element's attribute for both values and text content.
onclick	script	Optional. This event occurs when the user clicks on the user interface element.
ondblclick	script	Optional. This event occurs when the user double-clicks on the user interface element.
onkeydown	script	Optional. This event occurs when the user presses the specified key down on the user interface element.
onkeypress	script	Optional. This event occurs when the user presses and releases a key on the user interface element.

onkeyup	script	Optional. This event occurs when the user releases a key on the user interface element.
onmousedown	script	Optional. This event occurs when the user presses over the user interface element.
onmousemove	script	Optional. This event occurs when the user moves over the user interface element.
onmouseout	script	Optional. This event occurs when the user moves away from the user interface element.
onmouseover	script	Optional. This event occurs when the user moves over the user interface element.
onmouseup	script	Optional. This event occurs when the user releases the button over the user interface element.
style	style_definition	Optional. Specifies style information for the current element.
title	tooltip_text	Optional. Displays information about the specified element to which it is attached.

<cite>

Description:
The value of this attribute is a URI that designates a source document or message and usually is rendered as italics by the browser. This attribute is intended to point to information explaining why a document was changed.

Requires closing tag:
Yes

Attributes:

NAME	VALUE	DESCRIPTION
class	class_rule or style_rule	Optional. Assigns a class name or set of class names to an element.
dir	ltr or rtl	Optional. Sets the text direction to LTR (*Left To Right*) or RTL (*Right To Left*).
id	id_name	Optional. This attribute assigns a name to an element. This name must be unique within the document.
lang	language_code	Optional. Specifies the base language of an element's attribute for both values and text content.
onclick	script	Optional. This event occurs when the user clicks on the user interface element.
ondblclick	script	Optional. This event occurs when the user double-clicks on the user interface element.
onkeydown	script	Optional. This event occurs when the user presses the specified key down on the user interface element.
onkeypress	script	Optional. This event occurs when the user presses and

		releases a key on the user interface element.
onkeyup	script	Optional. This event occurs when the user releases a key on the user interface element.
onmousedown	script	Optional. This event occurs when the user presses over the user interface element.
onmousemove	script	Optional. This event occurs when the user moves over the user interface element.
onmouseout	script	Optional. This event occurs when the user moves away from the user interface element.
onmouseover	script	Optional. This event occurs when the user moves over the user interface element.
onmouseup	script	Optional. This event occurs when the user releases the button over the user interface element.
style	style_definition	Optional. Specifies style information for the current element.
title	tooltip_text	Optional. Displays information about the specified element to which it is attached.

See also:
`<ABBR>, <ACRONYM>, <CODE>, <DFN>, <EM>, <KBD>, <SAMP>, <STRONG>, <VAR>`

<code>

Description:
Using CODE to enclose text indicates that what is enclosed is source code; most often HTML tags and is rendered as a monospaced font.

Requires closing tag:
Yes

Attributes:

NAME	VALUE	DESCRIPTION
class	class_rule or style_rule	Optional. Assigns a class name or set of class names to an element.
dir	ltr or rtl	Optional. Sets the text direction to LTR (*Left To Right*) or RTL (*Right To Left*).
id	id_name	Optional. This attribute assigns a name to an element. This name must be unique within the document.
lang	language_code	Optional. Specifies the base language of an element's attribute for both values and text content.
onclick	script	Optional. This event occurs when the user clicks on the user interface element.
ondblclick	script	Optional. This event occurs when the user double-clicks on the user interface element.
onkeydown	script	Optional. This event occurs when the user presses the specified key down on the user interface element.
onkeypress	script	Optional. This event occurs when the user presses and releases a key on the user

		interface element.
onkeyup	script	Optional. This event occurs when the user releases a key on the user interface element.
onmousedown	script	Optional. This event occurs when the user presses over the user interface element.
onmousemove	script	Optional. This event occurs when the user moves over the user interface element.
onmouseout	script	Optional. This event occurs when the user moves away from the user interface element.
onmouseover	script	Optional. This event occurs when the user moves over the user interface element.
onmouseup	script	Optional. This event occurs when the user releases the button over the user interface element.
style	style_definition	Optional. Specifies style information for the current element.
title	tooltip_text	Optional. Displays information about the specified element to which it is attached.

See also:
`<ABBR>, <ACRONYM>, <CITE>, <DFN>, <EM>, <KBD>, <SAMP>, <STRONG>, <VAR>`

<col>

Description:
When it is necessary to single out a column (e.g., for style information, to specify width information, etc.) within a group, authors must identify that column with a `COL` element.

Requires closing tag:
No

Attributes:

NAME	VALUE	DESCRIPTION
align	right, left, center, justify, char	Optional. Specifies the alignment of data and the justification of text in a cell.
char	character	Optional. Specifies a single character within a text fragment to act as an axis for alignment.
charoff	pixels, %	Optional. Specifies the offset to the first occurrence of the alignment character on each line.
class	class_rule or style_rule	Optional. Assigns a class name or set of class names to an element.
dir	ltr or rtl	Optional. Sets the text direction to LTR (*Left To Right*) or RTL (*Right To Left*).
id	id_name	Optional. This attribute assigns a name to an element. This name must be unique within the document.
lang	language_code	Optional. Specifies the base language of an element's attribute for both values and text content.
onclick	script	Optional. This event occurs when the user clicks on the user interface element.

ondblclick	script	Optional. This event occurs when the user double-clicks on the user interface element.
onkeydown	script	Optional. This event occurs when the user presses the specified key down on the user interface element.
onkeypress	script	Optional. This event occurs when the user presses and releases a key on the user interface element.
onkeyup	script	Optional. This event occurs when the user releases a key on the user interface element.
onmousedown	script	Optional. This event occurs when the user presses over the user interface element.
onmousemove	script	Optional. This event occurs when the user moves over the user interface element.
onmouseout	script	Optional. This event occurs when the user moves away from the user interface element.
onmouseover	script	Optional. This event occurs when the user moves over the user interface element.
onmouseup	script	Optional. This event occurs when the user releases the button over the user interface element.
span	number	Optional. This attribute, whose value must be an integer of 0, specifies the number of columns spanned by the COL element.
style	style_definition	Optional. Specifies style information for the current element.
title	tooltip_text	Optional. Displays information about the specified element to which it is attached.
valign	top, middle, bottom, baseline	Optional. This attribute specifies the alignment of data and the justification of text in a cell.
width	%, pixels, relative_length	Optional. Specifies a default

		width for each column spanned by the current COL element.

See also:
<CAPTION>, <COLGROUP>, <TABLE>, <TBODY>, <TD>, <TFOOT>, <TH>, <THEAD>, <TR>

<colgroup>

Description:
A table may either contain a single implicit column group (no `COLGROUP` element delimits the columns) or any number of explicit column groups (each delimited by an instance of the `COLGROUP` element).

Requires closing tag:
No

Attributes:

NAME	VALUE	DESCRIPTION
align	right, left, center, justify, char	Optional. Specifies the alignment of data and the justification of text in a cell.
char	character	Optional. Specifies a single character within a text fragment to act as an axis for alignment.
charoff	pixels, %	Optional. Specifies the offset to the first occurrence of the alignment character on each line.
class	class_rule or style_rule	Optional. Assigns a class name or set of class names to an element.
dir	ltr or rtl	Optional. Sets the text direction to LTR (*Left To Right*) or RTL (*Right To Left*).
id	id_name	Optional. This attribute assigns a name to an element. This name must be unique within the document.
lang	language_code	Optional. Specifies the base language of an element's attribute for both values and text content.
onclick	script	Optional. This event occurs when the user clicks on the user interface element.

ondblclick	script	Optional. This event occurs when the user double-clicks on the user interface element.
onkeydown	script	Optional. This event occurs when the user presses the specified key down on the user interface element.
onkeypress	script	Optional. This event occurs when the user presses and releases a key on the user interface element.
onkeyup	script	Optional. This event occurs when the user releases a key on the user interface element.
onmousedown	script	Optional. This event occurs when the user presses over the user interface element.
onmousemove	script	Optional. This event occurs when the user moves over the user interface element.
onmouseout	script	Optional. This event occurs when the user moves away from the user interface element.
onmouseover	script	Optional. This event occurs when the user moves over the user interface element.
onmouseup	script	Optional. This event occurs when the user releases the button over the user interface element.
span	number	Optional. This attribute, which must be an integer of 0, specifies the number of columns in a column group.
style	style_definition	Optional. Specifies style information for the current element.
title	tooltip_text	Optional. Displays information about the specified element to which it is attached.
valign	top, middle, bottom, baseline	Optional. Specifies the alignment of data and the justification of text in a cell.
width	%, pixels, relative_length	Optional. Specifies a default width for each column in the current column group. This

		attribute allows the special form "0*" (zero asterisk) which means that the width of the each column in the group should be the minimum width necessary to hold the column's contents.

See also:
`<CAPTION>, <COL>, <TABLE>, <TBODY>, <TD>, <TFOOT>, <TH>, <THEAD>, <TR>`

<dd>

Description:
Definition lists vary only slightly from other types of lists in that list items consist of two parts: a term and a description. The term is given by the DT element and is restricted to inline content. The description is given with a DD element that contains block-level content.

Requires closing tag:
Yes

Attributes:

NAME	VALUE	DESCRIPTION
class	class_rule or style_rule	Optional. Assigns a class name or set of class names to an element.
dir	ltr or rtl	Optional. Sets the text direction to LTR (*Left To Right*) or RTL (*Right To Left*).
id	id_name	Optional. This attribute assigns a name to an element. This name must be unique within the document.
lang	language_code	Optional. Specifies the base language of an element's attribute for both values and text content.
onclick	script	Optional. This event occurs when the user clicks on the user interface element.
ondblclick	script	Optional. This event occurs when the user double-clicks on the user interface element.
onkeydown	script	Optional. This event occurs when the user presses the specified key down on the user interface element.
onkeypress	script	Optional. This event occurs when the user presses and

		releases a key on the user interface element.
onkeyup	script	Optional. This event occurs when the user releases a key on the user interface element.
onmousedown	script	Optional. This event occurs when the user presses over the user interface element.
onmousemove	script	Optional. This event occurs when the user moves over the user interface element.
onmouseout	script	Optional. This event occurs when the user moves away from the user interface element.
onmouseover	script	Optional. This event occurs when the user moves over the user interface element.
onmouseup	script	Optional. This event occurs when the user releases the button over the user interface element.
style	style_definition	Optional. Specifies style information for the current element.
title	tooltip_text	Optional. Displays information about the specified element to which it is attached.

See also:
`<DL>`, `<DT>`

<del>

Description:
INS and DEL are used to markup sections of the document that have been inserted or deleted with respect to a different version of a document (e.g., in draft legislation where lawmakers need to view the changes). These two elements are unusual for HTML in that they may serve as either block-level or inline elements (but not both). They may contain one or more words within a paragraph or contain one or more block-level elements such as paragraphs, lists and tables.

Requires closing tag:
Yes

Attributes:

NAME	VALUE	DESCRIPTION
cite	URL	Optional. This attribute is intended to point to information explaining why a document was changed.
class	class_rule or style_rule	Optional. Assigns a class name or set of class names to an element.
datetime	YYYYMMDD	Optional. Specifies the date and time when the change was made.
dir	ltr or rtl	Optional. Sets the text direction to LTR (*Left To Right*) or RTL (*Right To Left*).
id	id_name	Optional. This attribute assigns a name to an element. This name must be unique within the document.
lang	language_code	Optional. Specifies the base language of an element's attribute for both values and text content.
onclick	script	Optional. This event occurs when the user clicks on the user interface element.

ondblclick	script	Optional. This event occurs when the user double-clicks on the user interface element.
onkeydown	script	Optional. This event occurs when the user presses the specified key down on the user interface element.
onkeypress	script	Optional. This event occurs when the user presses and releases a key on the user interface element.
onkeyup	script	Optional. This event occurs when the user releases a key on the user interface element.
onmousedown	script	Optional. This event occurs when the user presses over the user interface element.
onmousemove	script	Optional. This event occurs when the user moves over the user interface element.
onmouseout	script	Optional. This event occurs when the user moves away from the user interface element.
onmouseover	script	Optional. This event occurs when the user moves over the user interface element.
onmouseup	script	Optional. This event occurs when the user releases the button over the user interface element.
style	style_definition	Optional. Specifies style information for the current element.
title	tooltip_text	Optional. Displays information about the specified element to which it is attached.

See also:
`<INS>, <CITE>`

<dfn>

Description:
Indicates that this is the defining instance of the enclosed term and is usually rendered as either bold italic or italic text.

Requires closing tag:
Yes

Attributes:

NAME	VALUE	DESCRIPTION
class	class_rule or style_rule	Optional. Assigns a class name or set of class names to an element.
dir	ltr or rtl	Optional. Sets the text direction to LTR (*Left To Right*) or RTL (*Right To Left*).
id	id_name	Optional. This attribute assigns a name to an element. This name must be unique within the document.
lang	language_code	Optional. Specifies the base language of an element's attribute for both values and text content.
onclick	script	Optional. This event occurs when the user clicks on the user interface element.
ondblclick	script	Optional. This event occurs when the user double-clicks on the user interface element.
onkeydown	script	Optional. This event occurs when the user presses the specified key down on the user interface element.
onkeypress	script	Optional. This event occurs when the user presses and releases a key on the user

		interface element.
onkeyup	script	Optional. This event occurs when the user releases a key on the user interface element.
onmousedown	script	Optional. This event occurs when the user presses over the user interface element.
onmousemove	script	Optional. This event occurs when the user moves over the user interface element.
onmouseout	script	Optional. This event occurs when the user moves away from the user interface element.
onmouseover	script	Optional. This event occurs when the user moves over the user interface element.
onmouseup	script	Optional. This event occurs when the user releases the button over the user interface element.
style	style_definition	Optional. Specifies style information for the current element.
title	tooltip_text	Optional. Displays information about the specified element to which it is attached.

See also:
`<ABBR>, <ACRONYM>, <CITE>, <CODE>, <EM>, <KBD>, <SAMP>, <STRONG>, <VAR>`

<dir>

Description:
The DIR element was designed to be used for creating multicolumn directory lists. The MENU element was designed to be used for single column menu lists. Both elements have the same structure as UL, just different rendering. In practice, a user agent will render a DIR or MENU list exactly as a UL list.

Requires closing tag:
Yes

Attributes:

NAME	VALUE	DESCRIPTION
class	class_rule or style_rule	Optional. Assigns a class name or set of class names to an element.
compact	compact_rendering	**Deprecated.** Optional This attribute allows visual user agents to render the list in a more compact way.
dir	ltr or rtl	Optional. Sets the text direction to LTR (*Left To Right*) or RTL (*Right To Left*).
id	id_name	Optional. This attribute assigns a name to an element. This name must be unique within the document.
lang	language_code	Optional. Specifies the base language of an element's attribute for both values and text content.
onclick	script	Optional. This event occurs when the user clicks on the user interface element.
ondblclick	script	Optional. This event occurs when the user double-clicks on the user interface element.
onkeydown	script	Optional. This event occurs when the user presses the

		specified key down on the user interface element.
onkeypress	script	Optional. This event occurs when the user presses and releases a key on the user interface element.
onkeyup	script	Optional. This event occurs when the user releases a key on the user interface element.
onmousedown	script	Optional. This event occurs when the user presses over the user interface element.
onmousemove	script	Optional. This event occurs when the user moves over the user interface element.
onmouseout	script	Optional. This event occurs when the user moves away from the user interface element.
onmouseover	script	Optional. This event occurs when the user moves over the user interface element.
onmouseup	script	Optional. This event occurs when the user releases the button over the user interface element.
style	style_definition	Optional. Specifies style information for the current element.
title	tooltip_text	Optional. Displays information about the specified element to which it is attached.

See also:
`<LI>, <MENU>, <OL>, <UL>`

<div>

Description:
The DIV and SPAN elements, in conjunction with the id and class attributes, offer a generic mechanism for adding structure to documents. These elements define content to be inline (SPAN) or block-level (DIV) but impose no other presentational idioms on the content. Thus, authors may use these elements in conjunction with style sheets, the lang attribute, etc., to tailor HTML to their own needs and tastes.

Requires closing tag:
Yes

Attributes:

NAME	VALUE	DESCRIPTION
align	left, right, center, justify	**Deprecated.** Optional. This attribute specifies the horizontal alignment of its element with respect to the surrounding context.
class	class_rule or style_rule	Optional. Assigns a class name or set of class names to an element.
dir	ltr or rtl	Optional. Sets the text direction to LTR (*Left To Right*) or RTL (*Right To Left*).
id	id_name	Optional. This attribute assigns a name to an element. This name must be unique within the document.
lang	language_code	Optional. Specifies the base language of an element's attribute for both values and text content.
onclick	script	Optional. This event occurs when the user clicks on the user interface element.
ondblclick	script	Optional. This event occurs when the user double-clicks on

		the user interface element.
onkeydown	script	Optional. This event occurs when the user presses the specified key down on the user interface element.
onkeypress	script	Optional. This event occurs when the user presses and releases a key on the user interface element.
onkeyup	script	Optional. This event occurs when the user releases a key on the user interface element.
onmousedown	script	Optional. This event occurs when the user presses over the user interface element.
onmousemove	script	Optional. This event occurs when the user moves over the user interface element.
onmouseout	script	Optional. This event occurs when the user moves away from the user interface element.
onmouseover	script	Optional. This event occurs when the user moves over the user interface element.
onmouseup	script	Optional. This event occurs when the user releases the button over the user interface element.
style	style_definition	Optional. Specifies style information for the current element.
title	tooltip_text	Optional. Displays information about the specified element to which it is attached.

See also:
`<SPAN>`

<dl>

Description:
Definition lists vary only slightly from other types of lists in that list items consist of two parts: a term and a description. The term is given by the DT element and is restricted to inline content. The description is given with a DD element that contains block-level content.

Requires closing tag:
Yes

Attributes:

NAME	VALUE	DESCRIPTION
class	class_rule or style_rule	Optional. Assigns a class name or set of class names to an element.
dir	ltr or rtl	Optional. Sets the text direction to LTR (*Left To Right*) or RTL (*Right To Left*).
id	id_name	Optional. This attribute assigns a name to an element. This name must be unique within the document.
lang	language_code	Optional. Specifies the base language of an element's attribute for both values and text content.
onclick	script	Optional. This event occurs when the user clicks on the user interface element.
ondblclick	script	Optional. This event occurs when the user double-clicks on the user interface element.
onkeydown	script	Optional. This event occurs when the user presses the specified key down on the user interface element.
onkeypress	script	Optional. This event occurs when the user presses and

		releases a key on the user interface element.
onkeyup	script	Optional. This event occurs when the user releases a key on the user interface element.
onmousedown	script	Optional. This event occurs when the user presses over the user interface element.
onmousemove	script	Optional. This event occurs when the user moves over the user interface element.
onmouseout	script	Optional. This event occurs when the user moves away from the user interface element.
onmouseover	script	Optional. This event occurs when the user moves over the user interface element.
onmouseup	script	Optional. This event occurs when the user releases the button over the user interface element.
style	style_definition	Optional. Specifies style information for the current element.
title	tooltip_text	Optional. Displays information about the specified element to which it is attached.

See also:
`<DD>, <DT>`

<dt>

Description:
Definition lists vary only slightly from other types of lists in that list items consist of two parts: a term and a description. The term is given by the DT element and is restricted to inline content. The description is given with a DD element that contains block-level content.

Requires closing tag:
Yes

Attributes:

NAME	VALUE	DESCRIPTION
class	class_rule or style_rule	Optional. Assigns a class name or set of class names to an element.
dir	ltr or rtl	Optional. Sets the text direction to LTR (*Left To Right*) or RTL (*Right To Left*).
id	id_name	Optional. This attribute assigns a name to an element. This name must be unique within the document.
lang	language_code	Optional. Specifies the base language of an element's attribute for both values and text content.
onclick	script	Optional. This event occurs when the user clicks on the user interface element.
ondblclick	script	Optional. This event occurs when the user double-clicks on the user interface element.
onkeydown	script	Optional. This event occurs when the user presses the specified key down on the user interface element.
onkeypress	script	Optional. This event occurs when the user presses and

		releases a key on the user interface element.
onkeyup	script	Optional. This event occurs when the user releases a key on the user interface element.
onmousedown	script	Optional. This event occurs when the user presses over the user interface element.
onmousemove	script	Optional. This event occurs when the user moves over the user interface element.
onmouseout	script	Optional. This event occurs when the user moves away from the user interface element.
onmouseover	script	Optional. This event occurs when the user moves over the user interface element.
onmouseup	script	Optional. This event occurs when the user releases the button over the user interface element.
style	style_definition	Optional. Specifies style information for the current element.
title	tooltip_text	Optional. Displays information about the specified element to which it is attached.

See also:
`<DD>, <DL>`

<em>

Description:
Phrase elements add structural information to text fragments. EM defines emphasized text.

Requires closing tag:
Yes

Attributes:

NAME	VALUE	DESCRIPTION
class	class_rule or style_rule	Optional. Assigns a class name or set of class names to an element.
dir	ltr or rtl	Optional. Sets the text direction to LTR (*Left To Right*) or RTL (*Right To Left*).
id	id_name	Optional. This attribute assigns a name to an element. This name must be unique within the document.
lang	language_code	Optional. Specifies the base language of an element's attribute for both values and text content.
onclick	script	Optional. This event occurs when the user clicks on the user interface element.
ondblclick	script	Optional. This event occurs when the user double-clicks on the user interface element.
onkeydown	script	Optional. This event occurs when the user presses the specified key down on the user interface element.
onkeypress	script	Optional. This event occurs when the user presses and releases a key on the user interface element.

onkeyup	script	Optional. This event occurs when the user releases a key on the user interface element.
onmousedown	script	Optional. This event occurs when the user presses over the user interface element.
onmousemove	script	Optional. This event occurs when the user moves over the user interface element.
onmouseout	script	Optional. This event occurs when the user moves away from the user interface element.
onmouseover	script	Optional. This event occurs when the user moves over the user interface element.
onmouseup	script	Optional. This event occurs when the user releases the button over the user interface element.
style	style_definition	Optional. Specifies style information for the current element.
title	tooltip_text	Optional. Displays information about the specified element to which it is attached.

See also:
`<ABBR>, <ACRONYM>, <CITE>, <CODE>, <DFN>, <KBD>, <SAMP>, <STRONG>, <VAR>`

<fieldset>

Description:
The `FIELDSET` element allows authors to group thematically related controls and labels. Grouping controls makes it easier for users to understand their purpose while simultaneously facilitating tabbing navigation for visual user agents and speech navigation for speech-oriented user agents. The proper use of this element makes documents more accessible.

Requires closing tag:
Yes

Attributes:

NAME	VALUE	DESCRIPTION
class	class_rule or style_rule	Optional. Assigns a class name or set of class names to an element.
dir	ltr or rtl	Optional. Sets the text direction to LTR (*Left To Right*) or RTL (*Right To Left*).
id	id_name	Optional. This attribute assigns a name to an element. This name must be unique within the document.
lang	language_code	Optional. Specifies the base language of an element's attribute for both values and text content.
onclick	script	Optional. This event occurs when the user clicks on the user interface element.
ondblclick	script	Optional. This event occurs when the user double-clicks on the user interface element.
onkeydown	script	Optional. This event occurs when the user presses the specified key down on the user interface element.
onkeypress	script	Optional. This event occurs

		when the user presses and releases a key on the user interface element.
onkeyup	script	Optional. This event occurs when the user releases a key on the user interface element.
onmousedown	script	Optional. This event occurs when the user presses over the user interface element.
onmousemove	script	Optional. This event occurs when the user moves over the user interface element.
onmouseout	script	Optional. This event occurs when the user moves away from the user interface element.
onmouseover	script	Optional. This event occurs when the user moves over the user interface element.
onmouseup	script	Optional. This event occurs when the user releases the button over the user interface element.
style	style_definition	Optional. Specifies style information for the current element.
title	tooltip_text	Optional. Displays information about the specified element to which it is attached.

See also:
`<FORM>, <INPUT>, <LABEL>, <LEGEND>, <TEXTAREA>`

<font>

Description:
Deprecated. The `FONT` element changes the font size and color for text in its contents.

Requires closing tag:
Yes

Attributes:

NAME	VALUE	DESCRIPTION
class	class_rule or style_rule	Optional. Assigns a class name or set of class names to an element.
color	rgb(x,x,x), #xxxxxx, colorname	**Deprecated**. Optional. This attribute sets the text color.
dir	ltr or rtl	Optional. Sets the text direction to LTR (*Left To Right*) or RTL (*Right To Left*).
face	list_of_fontnames	**Deprecated.** Optional. Defines a list of font names the user agent should search for in order of preference.
id	id_name	Optional. This attribute assigns a name to an element. This name must be unique within the document.
lang	language_code	Optional. Specifies the base language of an element's attribute for both values and text content.
onclick	script	Optional. This event occurs when the user clicks on the user interface element.
ondblclick	script	Optional. This event occurs when the user double-clicks on the user interface element.
onkeydown	script	Optional. This event occurs when the user presses the

		specified key down on the user interface element.
onkeypress	script	Optional. This event occurs when the user presses and releases a key on the user interface element.
onkeyup	script	Optional. This event occurs when the user releases a key on the user interface element.
onmousedown	script	Optional. This event occurs when the user presses over the user interface element.
onmousemove	script	Optional. This event occurs when the user moves over the user interface element.
onmouseout	script	Optional. This event occurs when the user moves away from the user interface element.
onmouseover	script	Optional. This event occurs when the user moves over the user interface element.
onmouseup	script	Optional. This event occurs when the user releases the button over the user interface element.
size	A number from 1 to 7. If basefont is specified you can specify a number from -6 to 6	**Deprecated.** Optional. This attribute sets the size of the font.
style	style_definition	Optional. Specifies style information for the current element.
title	tooltip_text	Optional. Displays information about the specified element to which it is attached.

See also:
`<BASEFONT>`

<form>

Description:
An HTML form is a section of a document containing normal content, markup, special elements called *controls* (checkboxes, radio buttons, menus, etc.), and labels on those controls. Users generally "complete" a form by modifying its controls (entering text, selecting menu items, etc.), before submitting the form to an agent for processing (e.g., to a Web server, to a mail server, etc.).

Requires closing tag:
Yes

Attributes:

NAME	VALUE	DESCRIPTION
accept	list of contenttypes	Optional. Specifies a comma-separated list of content types that a server processing the form will handle.
accept-charset	charset_list	Optional. Specifies the list of character encodings for input data that is accepted by the server processing the form.
action	URL	Required. Specifies a form processing agent. User agent behavior for a value other than an HTTP URI is undefined.
class	class_rule or style_rule	Optional. Assigns a class name or set of class names to an element.
dir	ltr or rtl	Optional. Sets the text direction to LTR (*Left To Right*) or RTL (*Right To Left*).
enctype	mimetype	Optional. This attribute specifies the content type used to submit the form to the server.
id	id_name	Optional. This attribute assigns a name to an element. This name must be unique within the document.

lang	language_code	Optional. Specifies the base language of an element's attribute for both values and text content.
method	get, post	Required. Specifies which HTTP method will be used to submit the form data set.
name	form_name	Optional. This attribute names the element so that it may be referred to from style sheets or scripts.
onclick	script	Optional. This event occurs when the user clicks on the user interface element.
ondblclick	script	Optional. This event occurs when the user double-clicks on the user interface element.
onkeydown	script	Optional. This event occurs when the user presses the specified key down on the user interface element.
onkeypress	script	Optional. This event occurs when the user presses and releases a key on the user interface element.
onkeyup	script	Optional. This event occurs when the user releases a key on the user interface element.
onmousedown	script	Optional. This event occurs when the user presses over the user interface element.
onmousemove	script	Optional. This event occurs when the user moves over the user interface element.
onmouseout	script	Optional. This event occurs when the user moves away from the user interface element.
onmouseover	script	Optional. This event occurs when the user moves over the user interface element.
onmouseup	script	Optional. This event occurs when the user releases the button over the user interface element.
style	style_definition	Optional. Specifies style information for the current

		element.
target	_blank, _self, _parent, _top	Optional. This attribute specifies the name of the frame where the document is opened.
title	tooltip_text	Optional. Displays information about the specified element to which it is attached.
type	Text, password, checkbox, radio, submit, reset, file, hidden, image, button	Required. Specifies the type of control to create.

See also:
`<FIELDSET>, <INPUT>, <LABEL>, <LEGEND>, <TEXTAREA>`

<frame>

Description:
HTML frames allow authors to present documents in multiple views, which may be independent windows or subwindows.

Requires closing tag:
Yes

Attributes:

NAME	VALUE	DESCRIPTION
class	class_rule or style_rule	Optional. Assigns a class name or set of class names to an element.
frameborder	0, 1	Optional. Provides the user agent with information about the frame border.
id	id_name	Optional. This attribute assigns a name to an element. This name must be unique within the document.
longdesc	URL	Optional. Specifies a link to a long description of the image and can be used to supplement the short description provided using the `alt` attribute.
marginheight	pixels	Optional. Specifies the amount of space between the frame's contents in its top and bottom margins.
marginwidth	pixels	Optional. Specifies the amount of space between the frame's contents in its left and right margins.
name	frame_name	Optional. This attribute assigns a name to the current frame. This name may be used as the target of subsequent links.

noresize	noresize	Optional. Tells the user agent that the frame window must not be resizeable.
scrolling	yes, no, auto	Optional. Specifies scroll information for the frame window.
src	URL	Optional. This attribute specifies the initial document the frame will contain.
style	style_definition	Optional. Specifies style information for the current element.
target	frame_target	Optional. This attribute specifies the name of the frame where the document is opened.
title	tooltip_text	Optional. Displays information about the specified element to which it is attached.

See also:
`<FRAMESET>, <IFRAME>, <NOFRAMES>, <OBJECT>`

<frameset>

Description:
The FRAMESET section of a document specifies the layout of views in the main user agent window. In addition, the FRAMESET section can contain a NOFRAMES element to provide alternate content for user agents that do not support frames or are configured not to display frames.

Requires closing tag:
Yes

Attributes:

NAME	VALUE	DESCRIPTION
class	class_rule or style_rule	Optional. Assigns a class name or set of class names to an element.
cols	pixels, %, *	Optional. Specifies the layout of vertical frames in a comma-separated list.
id	id_name	Optional. This attribute assigns a name to an element. This name must be unique within the document.
rows	pixels, %, *	Optional. Specifies the layout of horizontal frames in a comma-separated list.
style	style_definition	Optional. Specifies style information for the current element.
title	tooltip_text	Optional. Displays information about the specified element to which it is attached.

See also:
<FRAME>, <IFRAME>, <NOFRAMES>, <OBJECT>

<h1> to <h6>

Description:
There are six levels of headings in HTML with `H1` as the most important and `H6` as the least. Visual browsers usually render more important headings in larger fonts than less important ones.

Requires closing tag:
Yes

Attributes:

NAME	VALUE	DESCRIPTION
align	left, center, right, justify	**Deprecated.** Optional. This attribute specifies the horizontal alignment of its element with respect to the surrounding context.
class	class_rule or style_rule	Optional. Assigns a class name or set of class names to an element.
dir	ltr or rtl	Optional. Sets the text direction to LTR (*Left To Right*) or RTL (*Right To Left*).
id	id_name	Optional. This attribute assigns a name to an element. This name must be unique within the document.
lang	language_code	Optional. Specifies the base language of an element's attribute for both values and text content.
onclick	script	Optional. This event occurs when the user clicks on the user interface element.
ondblclick	script	Optional. This event occurs when the user double-clicks on the user interface element.
onkeydown	script	Optional. This event occurs when the user presses the

		specified key down on the user interface element.
onkeypress	script	Optional. This event occurs when the user presses and releases a key on the user interface element.
onkeyup	script	Optional. This event occurs when the user releases a key on the user interface element.
onmousedown	script	Optional. This event occurs when the user presses over the user interface element.
onmousemove	script	Optional. This event occurs when the user moves over the user interface element.
onmouseout	script	Optional. This event occurs when the user moves away from the user interface element.
onmouseover	script	Optional. This event occurs when the user moves over the user interface element.
onmouseup	script	Optional. This event occurs when the user releases the button over the user interface element.
style	style_definition	Optional. Specifies style information for the current element.
title	tooltip_text	Optional. Displays information about the specified element to which it is attached.

<head>

Description:
The HEAD element contains information about the current document, such as its title, keywords that may be useful to search engines, and other data that is not considered document content. User agents do not generally render elements that appear in the HEAD as content. They may, however, make information in the HEAD available to users through other mechanisms.

Requires closing tag:
Yes

Attributes:

NAME	VALUE	DESCRIPTION
dir	ltr or rtl	Optional. Sets the text direction to LTR (*Left To Right*) or RTL (*Right To Left*).
lang	language_code	Optional. Specifies the base language of an element's attribute for both values and text content.
profile	URL	Optional. This attribute specifies the location of one or more meta data profiles, separated by white space.

See also:
<BODY>, <HTML>, <META>, <TITLE>

<hr>

Description:
Deprecated. This attribute specifies the horizontal alignment of the rule with respect to the surrounding context.

Requires closing tag:
No

Attributes:

NAME	VALUE	DESCRIPTION
align	center, left, right	**Deprecated.** Optional. This attribute specifies the horizontal alignment of the rule with respect to the surrounding context.
class	class_rule or style_rule	Optional. Assigns a class name or set of class names to an element.
id	id_name	Optional. This attribute assigns a name to an element. This name must be unique within the document.
noshade	noshade	**Deprecated.** Optional. Renders the horrizontal rule with a solid color instead of with two colors.
onclick	script	Optional. This event occurs when the user clicks on the user interface element.
ondblclick	script	Optional. This event occurs when the user double-clicks on the user interface element.
onkeydown	script	Optional. This event occurs when the user presses the specified key down on the user interface element.
onkeypress	script	Optional. This event occurs when the user presses and

		releases a key on the user interface element.
onkeyup	script	Optional. This event occurs when the user releases a key on the user interface element.
onmousedown	script	Optional. This event occurs when the user presses over the user interface element.
onmousemove	script	Optional. This event occurs when the user moves over the user interface element.
onmouseout	script	Optional. This event occurs when the user moves away from the user interface element.
onmouseover	script	Optional. This event occurs when the user moves over the user interface element.
onmouseup	script	Optional. This event occurs when the user releases the button over the user interface element.
size	pixels, %	**Deprecated.** Optional. Specifies the height of the rule.
style	style_definition	Optional. Specifies style information for the current element.
title	tooltip_text	Optional. Displays information about the specified element to which it is attached.
width	pixels, %	**Deprecated.** Optional. This attribute specifies the width of the rule.

<html>

Description:
To publish information for global distribution, one needs a universally understood language, a kind of publishing mother tongue that all computers may potentially understand. The publishing language used by the World Wide Web is HTML (from HyperText Markup Language). `HTML` is used to begin the actual document.

Requires closing tag:
Yes

Attributes:

NAME	VALUE	DESCRIPTION
dir	ltr or rtl	Optional. Sets the text direction to LTR (*Left To Right*) or RTL (*Right To Left*).
lang	language_code	Optional. Specifies the base language of an element's attribute for both values and text content.
xmlns	http://www.w3.org/1999/xhtml	Required. Defines the XML namespace attribute

See also:
`<BODY>, <HEAD>, <META>, <TITLE>`

<i>

Description:
Sets text closed within `I` tags as italicized text.

Requires closing tag:
Yes

Attributes:

NAME	VALUE	DESCRIPTION
class	class_rule or style_rule	Optional. Assigns a class name or set of class names to an element.
dir	ltr or rtl	Optional. Sets the text direction to LTR (*Left To Right*) or RTL (*Right To Left*).
id	id_name	Optional. This attribute assigns a name to an element. This name must be unique within the document.
lang	language_code	Optional. Specifies the base language of an element's attribute for both values and text content.
onclick	script	Optional. This event occurs when the user clicks on the user interface element.
ondblclick	script	Optional. This event occurs when the user double-clicks on the user interface element.
onkeydown	script	Optional. This event occurs when the user presses the specified key down on the user interface element.
onkeypress	script	Optional. This event occurs when the user presses and releases a key on the user interface element.

onkeyup	script	Optional. This event occurs when the user releases a key on the user interface element.
onmousedown	script	Optional. This event occurs when the user presses over the user interface element.
onmousemove	script	Optional. This event occurs when the user moves over the user interface element.
onmouseout	script	Optional. This event occurs when the user moves away from the user interface element.
onmouseover	script	Optional. This event occurs when the user moves over the user interface element.
onmouseup	script	Optional. This event occurs when the user releases the button over the user interface element.
style	style_definition	Optional. Specifies style information for the current element.
title	tooltip_text	Optional. Displays information about the specified element.

See also:
`<B>, <BIG>, <S>, <SMALL>, <STRIKE>, <TT>, <U>`

<iframe>

Description:
The `IFRAME` element allows authors to insert a frame within a block of text. Inserting an inline frame within a section of text is much like inserting an object via the `OBJECT` element: they both allow you to insert an HTML document in the middle of another they may both be aligned with surrounding text, etc.

Requires closing tag:
Yes

Attributes:

NAME	VALUE	DESCRIPTION
align	left, right, top, middle, bottom	Optional. This attribute specifies how to align the iframe according to the surrounding text
class	class_rule or style_rule	Optional. Assigns a class name or set of class names to an element.
frameborder	1, 0	Optional. This attribute provides the user agent with information about the frame border.
height	pixels, %	Optional. Sets the height of the inline frame.
id	id_name	Optional. This attribute assigns a name to an element. This name must be unique within the document.
longdesc	URL	Optional. Specifies a link to a long description of the image.
marginheight	pixels	Optional. This attribute specifies the amount of space to be left between the frame's contents in its top and bottom margins.
marginwidth	pixels	Optional. This attribute specifies the amount of space to

		be left between the frame's contents in its left and right margins.
name	frame_name	Optional. Assigns a name to the current frame and may be used as the target of subsequent links.
scrolling	yes, no, auto	Optional. Specifies scroll information for the frame window.
src	URL	Optional. This attribute specifies the location of the contents within the frame.
style	style_definition	Optional. Specifies style information for the current element.
title	tooltip_text	Optional. Displays information about the specified element to which it is attached.
width	pixels, %	Optional. The width of the inline frame.

See also:
`<FRAME>, <FRAMESET>, <NOFRAMES>, <OBJECT>`

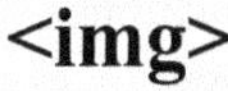

<img>

Description:
The `IMG` element defines an image.

Requires closing tag:
No

Attributes:

NAME	VALUE	DESCRIPTION
align	top, bottom, middle, left, right	**Deprecated.** Optional. This attribute specifies the position of an IMG, OBJECT, or APPLET.
alt	text	Optional. Specifies alternate text for user agents that cannot display images, forms, or applets.
border	pixels	**Deprecated.** Optional. This attribute specifies the width of an `IMG` or `OBJECT` border, in pixels.
class	class_rule or style_rule	Optional. Assigns a class name or set of class names to an element.
dir	ltr or rtl	Optional. Sets the text direction to LTR (*Left To Right*) or RTL (*Right To Left*).
height	pixels, %	Optional. Image and object height override.
hspace	pixels	**Deprecated.** Optional. This attribute specifies the amount of white space to be inserted to the left and right of an IMG, APPLET, or OBJECT.
id	id_name	Optional. This attribute assigns a name to an element. This name must be unique within the

		document.
ismap	URL	Optional. This attribute defines the image as a server-side image map.
lang	language_code	Optional. Specifies the base language of an element's attribute for both values and text content.
longdesc	URL	Optional. This attribute specifies a link to a long description of the image. This description should supplement the short description provided using the `alt` attribute.
name	Unique_name	Optional. This attribute names the element so that it may be referred to from style sheets or scripts.
onclick	script	Optional. This event occurs when the user clicks on the user interface element.
ondblclick	script	Optional. This event occurs when the user double-clicks on the user interface element.
onkeydown	script	Optional. This event occurs when the user presses the specified key down on the user interface element.
onkeypress	script	Optional. This event occurs when the user presses and releases a key on the user interface element.
onkeyup	script	Optional. This event occurs when the user releases a key on the user interface element.
onmousedown	script	Optional. This event occurs when the user presses over the user interface element.
onmousemove	script	Optional. This event occurs when the user moves over the user interface element.
onmouseout	script	Optional. This event occurs when the user moves away from the user interface element.
onmouseover	script	Optional. This event occurs when the user moves over the

		user interface element.
onmouseup	script	Optional. This event occurs when the user releases the button over the user interface element.
src	URL	Required. This attribute specifies the location of the image resource.
style	style_definition	Optional. Specifies style information for the current element.
title	tooltip_text	Optional. Displays information about the specified element to which it is attached.
usemap	URL	Optional. This attribute associates an image map with an element.
vspace	pixels	**Deprecated**. Optional. This attribute specifies the amount of white space to be inserted above and below an IMG, APPLET, or OBJECT.
width	pixels, %	Optional. Image and object width override.

<input>

Description:
The `input` tag defines the start of an input field where the user can enter data.

Requires closing tag:
Yes

Attributes:

NAME	VALUE	DESCRIPTION
accept	list_of_mime_types	Optional. Sets a comma-separated list of content types that a server processing this form will handle correctly.
accesskey	character	Optional. Allows the user to use keyboard keys for functions instead of a mouse.
align	left, right, top, texttop, middle, absmiddle, baseline, bottom, absbottom	**Deprecated.** Optional. This attribute specifies the position of an `IMG`, `OBJECT`, or `APPLET`.
alt	text	Optional. Specifies alternate text for user agents that cannot display images, forms, or applets.
checked	checked	Optional. Specifies that the button is on when the value is set to radio or checkbox.
class	class_rule or style_rule	Optional. Assigns a class name or set of class names to an element.
dir	ltr or rtl	Optional. Sets the text direction to LTR (*Left To Right*) or RTL (*Right To Left*).
disabled	disabled	Optional. Disables the control of user input.
id	id_name	Optional. This attribute assigns a name to an element. This

		name must be unique within the document.
lang	language_code	Optional. Specifies the base language of an element's attribute for both values and text content.
maxlength	number	Optional. When the `type` attribute has the value "text" or "password", this attribute specifies the maximum number of characters the user may enter.
name	field_name	Optional. This attribute assigns the control name.
onclick	script	Optional. This event occurs when the user clicks on the user interface element.
ondblclick	script	Optional. This event occurs when the user double-clicks on the user interface element.
onkeydown	script	Optional. This event occurs when the user presses the specified key down on the user interface element.
onkeypress	script	Optional. This event occurs when the user presses and releases a key on the user interface element.
onkeyup	script	Optional. This event occurs when the user releases a key on the user interface element.
onmousedown	script	Optional. This event occurs when the user presses over the user interface element.
onmousemove	script	Optional. This event occurs when the user moves over the user interface element.
onmouseout	script	Optional. This event occurs when the user moves away from the user interface element.
onmouseover	script	Optional. This event occurs when the user moves over the user interface element.
onmouseup	script	Optional. This event occurs when the user releases the button over the user interface

		element.
readonly	readonly	Optional. This attribute prohibits changes to the control.
size	number_of_char	Optional. This attribute sets the user agent the initial width of the control.
src	URL	Optional. When the `type` attribute has the value "image", this attribute specifies the location of the image to be used to decorate the graphical submit button.
style	style_definition	Optional. Specifies style information for the current element.
tabindex	number	Optional. This attribute specifies the position of the current element in the tabbing order for the current document.
title	tooltip_text	Optional. Displays information about the specified element to which it is attached.
type	button, checkbox, file, hidden, image, password, radio, reset, submit, text	Optional. This attribute specifies the type of control to create.
value	value	Optional. This attribute specifies the initial value of the control. It is optional except when the `type` attribute has the value "radio" or "checkbox".

See also:
`<FIELDSET>, <FORM>, <LABEL>, <LEGEND>, <TEXTAREA>`

<ins>

Description:
`INS` is used to markup sections of the document that have been inserted or deleted with respect to a different version of a document (e.g., in draft legislation where lawmakers need to view the changes).

Requires closing tag:
Yes

Attributes:

NAME	VALUE	DESCRIPTION
cite	URL	Optional. This attribute is intended to point to information explaining why a document was changed.
class	class_rule or style_rule	Optional. Assigns a class name or set of class names to an element.
datetime	YYYYMMDD	Optional. This attribute specifies the date and time when the change was made.
dir	ltr or rtl	Optional. Sets the text direction to LTR (*Left To Right*) or RTL (*Right To Left*).
id	id_name	Optional. This attribute assigns a name to an element. This name must be unique within the document.
lang	language_code	Optional. Specifies the base language of an element's attribute for both values and text content.
onclick	script	Optional. This event occurs when the user clicks on the user interface element.
ondblclick	script	Optional. This event occurs when the user double-clicks on the user interface element.

onkeydown	script	Optional. This event occurs when the user presses the specified key down on the user interface element.
onkeypress	script	Optional. This event occurs when the user presses and releases a key on the user interface element.
onkeyup	script	Optional. This event occurs when the user releases a key on the user interface element.
onmousedown	script	Optional. This event occurs when the user presses over the user interface element.
onmousemove	script	Optional. This event occurs when the user moves over the user interface element.
onmouseout	script	Optional. This event occurs when the user moves away from the user interface element.
onmouseover	script	Optional. This event occurs when the user moves over the user interface element.
onmouseup	script	Optional. This event occurs when the user releases the button over the user interface element.
style	style_definition	Optional. Specifies style information for the current element.
title	tooltip_text	Optional. Displays information about the specified element to which it is attached.

See also:
`<CITE>, <DEL>`

<kbd>

Description:
Phrase elements add structural information to text fragments. `KBD` indicates text to be entered by the user.

Requires closing tag:
No

Attributes:

NAME	VALUE	DESCRIPTION
class	class_rule or style_rule	Optional. Assigns a class name or set of class names to an element.
dir	ltr or rtl	Optional. Sets the text direction to LTR (*Left To Right*) or RTL (*Right To Left*).
id	id_name	Optional. This attribute assigns a name to an element. This name must be unique within the document.
lang	language_code	Optional. Specifies the base language of an element's attribute for both values and text content.
onclick	script	Optional. This event occurs when the user clicks on the user interface element.
ondblclick	script	Optional. This event occurs when the user double-clicks on the user interface element.
onkeydown	script	Optional. This event occurs when the user presses the specified key down on the user interface element.
onkeypress	script	Optional. This event occurs when the user presses and releases a key on the user interface element.

onkeyup	script	Optional. This event occurs when the user releases a key on the user interface element.
onmousedown	script	Optional. This event occurs when the user presses over the user interface element.
onmousemove	script	Optional. This event occurs when the user moves over the user interface element.
onmouseout	script	Optional. This event occurs when the user moves away from the user interface element.
onmouseover	script	Optional. This event occurs when the user moves over the user interface element.
onmouseup	script	Optional. This event occurs when the user releases the button over the user interface element.
style	style_definition	Optional. Specifies style information for the current element.
title	tooltip_text	Optional. Displays information about the specified element to which it is attached.

See also:
`<ABBR>, <ACRONYM>, <CITE>, <CODE>, <DFN>, <EM>, <SAMP>, <STRONG>, <VAR>`

<label>

Description:
The LABEL element may be used to attach information to controls. Each `LABEL` element is associated with exactly one form control.

Requires closing tag:
Yes

Attributes:

NAME	VALUE	DESCRIPTION
accesskey	character	Optional. Allows the user to use keyboard keys for functions instead of a mouse.
class	class_rule or style_rule	Optional. Assigns a class name or set of class names to an element.
dir	ltr or rtl	Optional. Sets the text direction to LTR (*Left To Right*) or RTL (*Right To Left*).
for	id_of_another_field	Optional. This attribute explicitly associates the label being defined with another control.
id	id_name	Optional. This attribute assigns a name to an element and must be unique within the document.
lang	language_code	Optional. Specifies the base language of an element's attribute for both values and text content.
onclick	script	Optional. This event occurs when the user clicks on the user interface element.
ondblclick	script	Optional. This event occurs when the user double-clicks on the user interface element.
onkeydown	script	Optional. This event occurs

		when the user presses the specified key down on the user interface element.
onkeypress	script	Optional. This event occurs when the user presses and releases a key on the user interface element.
onkeyup	script	Optional. This event occurs when the user releases a key on the user interface element.
onmousedown	script	Optional. This event occurs when the user presses over the user interface element.
onmousemove	script	Optional. This event occurs when the user moves over the user interface element.
onmouseout	script	Optional. This event occurs when the user moves away from the user interface element.
onmouseover	script	Optional. This event occurs when the user moves over the user interface element.
onmouseup	script	Optional. This event occurs when the user releases the button over the user interface element.
style	style_definition	Optional. Specifies style information for the current element.
title	tooltip_text	Optional. Displays information about the specified element to which it is attached.

See also:
`<FIELDSET>, <FORM>, <INPUT>, <LEGEND>, <TEXTAREA>`

<legend>

Description:
The `LEGEND` element allows authors to assign a caption to a `FIELDSET`. The legend improves accessibility when the `FIELDSET` is rendered non-visually.

Requires closing tag:
Yes

Attributes:

NAME	VALUE	DESCRIPTION
accesskey	character	Optional. Allows the user to use keyboard keys for functions instead of a mouse.
align	top, bottom, left, right	**Deprecated.** Optional. This attribute specifies the position of the legend with respect to the fieldset.
class	class_rule or style_rule	Optional. Assigns a class name or set of class names to an element.
dir	ltr or rtl	Optional. Sets the text direction to LTR (*Left To Right*) or RTL (*Right To Left*).
id	id_name	Optional. This attribute assigns a name to an element. This name must be unique within the document.
lang	language_code	Optional. Specifies the base language of an element's attribute for both values and text content.
onclick	script	Optional. This event occurs when the user clicks on the user interface element.
ondblclick	script	Optional. This event occurs when the user double-clicks on the user interface element.

onkeydown	script	Optional. This event occurs when the user presses the specified key down on the user interface element.
onkeypress	script	Optional. This event occurs when the user presses and releases a key on the user interface element.
onkeyup	script	Optional. This event occurs when the user releases a key on the user interface element.
onmousedown	script	Optional. This event occurs when the user presses over the user interface element.
onmousemove	script	Optional. This event occurs when the user moves over the user interface element.
onmouseout	script	Optional. This event occurs when the user moves away from the user interface element.
onmouseover	script	Optional. This event occurs when the user moves over the user interface element.
onmouseup	script	Optional. This event occurs when the user releases the button over the user interface element.
style	style_definition	Optional. Specifies style information for the current element.
title	tooltip_text	Optional. Displays information about the specified element to which it is attached.

See also:
`<FIELDSET>, <FORM>, <INPUT>, <LABEL>, <TEXTAREA>`

<li>

Description:
The LI tag defines the start of each list item in both ordered lists (<OL>) and unordered lists (<UL>).

Requires closing tag:
No

Attributes:

NAME	VALUE	DESCRIPTION
class	class_rule or style_rule	Optional. Assigns a class name or set of class names to an element.
dir	ltr or rtl	Optional. Sets the text direction to LTR (*Left To Right*) or RTL (*Right To Left*).
id	id_name	Optional. This attribute assigns a name to an element. This name must be unique within the document.
lang	language_code	Optional. Specifies the base language of an element's attribute for both values and text content.
onclick	script	Optional. This event occurs when the user clicks on the user interface element.
ondblclick	script	Optional. This event occurs when the user double-clicks on the user interface element.
onkeydown	script	Optional. This event occurs when the user presses the specified key down on the user interface element.
onkeypress	script	Optional. This event occurs when the user presses and releases a key on the user interface element.

onkeyup	script	Optional. This event occurs when the user releases a key on the user interface element.
onmousedown	script	Optional. This event occurs when the user presses over the user interface element.
onmousemove	script	Optional. This event occurs when the user moves over the user interface element.
onmouseout	script	Optional. This event occurs when the user moves away from the user interface element.
onmouseover	script	Optional. This event occurs when the user moves over the user interface element.
onmouseup	script	Optional. This event occurs when the user releases the button over the user interface element.
style	style_definition	Optional. Specifies style information for the current element.
title	tooltip_text	Optional. Displays information about the specified element to which it is attached.
type	A, a, I, i, 1, disc, square, circle	**Deprecated.** Optional. Sets the style of a list item.
value	number_of_list_item	**Deprecated.** Optional. Sets the number of the current list item.

See also:
`<DIR>, <MENU>, <OL>, <UL>`

<link>

Description:
This element defines a link. Unlike A, it may only appear in the HEAD section of a document, although it may appear any number of times. Although LINK has no content, it conveys relationship information that may be rendered by user agents in a variety of ways (e.g., a tool-bar with a drop-down menu of links).

Requires closing tag:
No

Attributes:

NAME	VALUE	DESCRIPTION
charset	charset	Optional. This attribute specifies the character encoding of the resource designated by the link.
class	class_rule or style_rule	Optional. Assigns a class name or set of class names to an element.
dir	ltr or rtl	Optional. Sets the text direction to LTR (*Left To Right*) or RTL (*Right To Left*).
href	URL	Optional. Specifies the location of a Web resource, which defines a link between the source and the destination.
hreflang	language_code	Optional. Specifies the base language of the resource designated by `href` and may only be used when `href` is specified.
id	id_name	Optional. This attribute assigns a name to an element. This name must be unique within the document.
lang	language_code	Optional. Specifies the base language of an element's attribute for both values and

		text content.
media	screen, tty, tv, projection, handheld, print, braille, aural, all	Optional. Specifies the intended medium for style information.
name	section_name	Optional. This attribute names the current anchor so that it may be the destination of another link. *In future versions of XHTML the name attribute will be replaced by the id attribute!*
onclick	script	Optional. This event occurs when the user clicks on the user interface element.
ondblclick	script	Optional. This event occurs when the user double-clicks on the user interface element.
onkeydown	script	Optional. This event occurs when the user presses the specified key down on the user interface element.
onkeypress	script	Optional. This event occurs when the user presses and releases a key on the user interface element.
onkeyup	script	Optional. This event occurs when the user releases a key on the user interface element.
onmousedown	script	Optional. This event occurs when the user presses over the user interface element.
onmousemove	script	Optional. This event occurs when the user moves over the user interface element.
onmouseout	script	Optional. This event occurs when the user moves away from the user interface element.
onmouseover	script	Optional. This event occurs when the user moves over the user interface element.
onmouseup	script	Optional. This event occurs when the user releases the button over the user interface element.
rel	alternate, appendix, bookmark, chapter, contents, copyright,	Optional. Specifies the forward link from the anchor specified

	glossary, help, home, index, next, prev, section, start, stylesheet, subsection	by the `href` attribute to the current document.
rev	alternate, appendix, bookmark, chapter, contents, copyright, glossary, help, home, index, next, prev, section, start, stylesheet, subsection	Optional. This attribute is used to describe a reverse link from the anchor specified by the `href` attribute to the current document.
style	style_definition	Optional. Specifies style information for the current element.
target	_blank, _self, _top, _parent	Optional. This attribute specifies the name of the frame where the document is opened.
title	tooltip_text	Optional. Displays information about the specified element to which it is attached.
type	MIME_type like:, text/css, text/javascript, image/gif	Optional. Sets the content type available for the target address.

<map>

Description:
The MAP element specifies a client-side image map (or other navigation mechanism) that may be associated with another elements (IMG, OBJECT, or INPUT).

Requires closing tag:
Yes

Attributes:

NAME	VALUE	DESCRIPTION
class	class_rule or style_rule	Optional. Assigns a class name or set of class names to an element.
dir	ltr or rtl	Optional. Sets the text direction to LTR (*Left To Right*) or RTL (*Right To Left*).
id	unique_name	Optional. This attribute defines a unique name for the map tag.
id	id_name	Optional. This attribute assigns a name to an element and must be unique within the document.
lang	language_code	Optional. Specifies the base language of an element's attribute for both values and text content.
name	unique_name	Optional. This attribute assigns a name to the image map defined by a MAP element.
onclick	script	Optional. This event occurs when the user clicks on the user interface element.
ondblclick	script	Optional. This event occurs when the user double-clicks on the user interface element.
onkeydown	script	Optional. This event occurs when the user presses the specified key down on the user

		interface element.
onkeypress	script	Optional. This event occurs when the user presses and releases a key on the user interface element.
onkeyup	script	Optional. This event occurs when the user releases a key on the user interface element.
onmousedown	script	Optional. This event occurs when the user presses over the user interface element.
onmousemove	script	Optional. This event occurs when the user moves over the user interface element.
onmouseout	script	Optional. This event occurs when the user moves away from the user interface element.
onmouseover	script	Optional. This event occurs when the user moves over the user interface element.
onmouseup	script	Optional. This event occurs when the user releases the button over the user interface element.
style	style_definition	Optional. Specifies style information for the current element.
title	tooltip_text	Optional. Displays information about the specified element to which it is attached.

<menu>

Description:
The MENU element was designed to be used for single column menu lists. This element has the same structure as UL, just different rendering.

Requires closing tag:
Yes

Attributes:

NAME	VALUE	DESCRIPTION
class	class_rule or style_rule	Optional. Assigns a class name or set of class names to an element.
compact	compact_rendering	**Deprecated.** Optional. Renders the list in a more compact way.
dir	ltr or rtl	Optional. Sets the text direction to LTR (*Left To Right*) or RTL (*Right To Left*).
id	id_name	Optional. This attribute assigns a name to an element. This name must be unique within the document.
lang	language_code	Optional. Specifies the base language of an element's attribute for both values and text content.
onclick	script	Optional. This event occurs when the user clicks on the user interface element.
ondblclick	script	Optional. This event occurs when the user double-clicks on the user interface element.
onkeydown	script	Optional. This event occurs when the user presses the specified key down on the user interface element.
onkeypress	script	Optional. This event occurs

		when the user presses and releases a key on the user interface element.
onkeyup	script	Optional. This event occurs when the user releases a key on the user interface element.
onmousedown	script	Optional. This event occurs when the user presses over the user interface element.
onmousemove	script	Optional. This event occurs when the user moves over the user interface element.
onmouseout	script	Optional. This event occurs when the user moves away from the user interface element.
onmouseover	script	Optional. This event occurs when the user moves over the user interface element.
onmouseup	script	Optional. This event occurs when the user releases the button over the user interface element.
style	style_definition	Optional. Specifies style information for the current element.
title	tooltip_text	Optional. Displays information about the specified element to which it is attached.

See also:
`<DIR>, <LI>, <OL>, <UL>`

<meta>

Description:
The `meta` element provides meta-information about `HTML` pages, such as descriptions and keywords for search engines and refresh rates.

Requires closing tag:
No

Attributes:

NAME	VALUE	DESCRIPTION
content	some_text	Required. This attribute specifies a property's value.
dir	ltr or rtl	Optional. Sets the text direction to LTR (*Left To Right*) or RTL (*Right To Left*).
http-equiv	content-type, expires, refresh, set-cookie	Optional. This attribute may be used in place of the `name` attribute.
lang	language_code	Optional. Specifies the base language of an element's attribute for both values and text content.
name	author, description, keywords, generator, revised	Optional. This attribute identifies a property name.
scheme	some_text	Optional. This attribute names a scheme to be used to interpret the property's value.

See also:
`<BODY>, <HEAD>, <HTML>, <TITLE>`

<noframes>

Description:
The NOFRAMES element specifies content that should be displayed only by user agents that do not support frames or are configured not to display frames. User agents that support frames must only display the contents of a NOFRAMES declaration when configured not to display frames. User agents that do not support frames must display the contents of NOFRAMES in any case.

Requires closing tag:
Yes

Attributes:

NAME	VALUE	DESCRIPTION
class	class_rule or style_rule	Optional. Assigns a class name or set of class names to an element.
dir	ltr or rtl	Optional. Sets the text direction to LTR (*Left To Right*) or RTL (*Right To Left*).
id	id_name	Optional. This attribute assigns a name to an element. This name must be unique within the document.
lang	language_code	Optional. Specifies the base language of an element's attribute for both values and text content.
onclick	script	Optional. This event occurs when the user clicks on the user interface element.
ondblclick	script	Optional. This event occurs when the user double-clicks on the user interface element.
onkeydown	script	Optional. This event occurs when the user presses the specified key down on the user interface element.
onkeypress	script	Optional. This event occurs

		when the user presses and releases a key on the user interface element.
onkeyup	script	Optional. This event occurs when the user releases a key on the user interface element.
onmousedown	script	Optional. This event occurs when the user presses over the user interface element.
onmousemove	script	Optional. This event occurs when the user moves over the user interface element.
onmouseout	script	Optional. This event occurs when the user moves away from the user interface element.
onmouseover	script	Optional. This event occurs when the user moves over the user interface element.
onmouseup	script	Optional. This event occurs when the user releases the button over the user interface element.
style	style_definition	Optional. Specifies style information for the current element.
title	tooltip_text	Optional. Displays information about the specified element to which it is attached.

See also:
`<FRAME>, <FRAMESET>, <IFRAME>, <OBJECT>`

<noscript>

Description:
The NOSCRIPT element allows authors to provide alternate content when a script is not executed. The content of a NOSCRIPT element should only be rendered by a script-aware user agent in the following cases:
The user agent is configured not to evaluate scripts.
The user agent doesn't support a scripting language invoked by a SCRIPT element earlier in the document.

Requires closing tag:
Yes

Attributes:

NAME	VALUE	DESCRIPTION
class	class_rule or style_rule	Optional. Assigns a class name or set of class names to an element.
dir	ltr or rtl	Optional. Sets the text direction to LTR (*Left To Right*) or RTL (*Right To Left*).
id	id_name	Optional. This attribute assigns a name to an element. This name must be unique within the document.
lang	language_code	Optional. Specifies the base language of an element's attribute for both values and text content.
onclick	script	Optional. This event occurs when the user clicks on the user interface element.
ondblclick	script	Optional. This event occurs when the user double-clicks on the user interface element.
onkeydown	script	Optional. This event occurs when the user presses the specified key down on the user

		interface element.
onkeypress	script	Optional. This event occurs when the user presses and releases a key on the user interface element.
onkeyup	script	Optional. This event occurs when the user releases a key on the user interface element.
onmousedown	script	Optional. This event occurs when the user presses over the user interface element.
onmousemove	script	Optional. This event occurs when the user moves over the user interface element.
onmouseout	script	Optional. This event occurs when the user moves away from the user interface element.
onmouseover	script	Optional. This event occurs when the user moves over the user interface element.
onmouseup	script	Optional. This event occurs when the user releases the button over the user interface element.
style	style_definition	Optional. Specifies style information for the current element.
title	tooltip_text	Optional. Displays information about the specified element to which it is attached.

See also:
`<SCRIPT>`

<object>

Description:
The OBJECT element allows authors to control whether data should be rendered externally or by some program, specified by the author, that renders the data within the user agent.

Requires closing tag:
Yes

Attributes:

NAME	VALUE	DESCRIPTION
align	left, right, top, bottom	**Deprecated.** Optional. This attribute specifies the position of an IMG, OBJECT, or APPLET.
archive	URL	Optional. Indicates whether or not the file has been updated since the last backup.
border	pixels	**Deprecated.** Optional. This attribute specifies the width of an IMG or OBJECT border, in pixels.
class	class_rule or style_rule	Optional. Assigns a class name or set of class names to an element.
classid	class ID	Optional. Identifies which plug-in to use.
codebase	URL	Optional. This attribute specifies the base path used to resolve relative URIs specified by the classid, data, and archive attributes.
codetype	MIME type	Optional. This attribute specifies the content type of data expected when downloading the object specified by classid.
data	URL	Optional. This attribute may be

		used to specify the location of the object's data.
declare	declare	Optional. Sets the current `OBJECT` definition a declaration only.
dir	ltr or rtl	Optional. Sets the text direction to LTR (*Left To Right*) or RTL (*Right To Left*).
height	pixels	Optional. Image and object height override.
hspace	pixels	**Deprecated**. Optional. This attribute specifies the amount of white space to be inserted to the left and right of an IMG, APPLET, or OBJECT.
id	id_name	Optional. This attribute assigns a name to an element. This name must be unique within the document.
lang	language_code	Optional. Specifies the base language of an element's attribute for both values and text content.
name	unique_name	Optional. This attribute defines a unique name for the object to use in scripts.
onclick	script	Optional. This event occurs when the user clicks on the user interface element.
ondblclick	script	Optional. This event occurs when the user double-clicks on the user interface element.
onkeydown	script	Optional. This event occurs when the user presses the specified key down on the user interface element.
onkeypress	script	Optional. This event occurs when the user presses and releases a key on the user interface element.
onkeyup	script	Optional. This event occurs when the user releases a key on the user interface element.
onmousedown	script	Optional. This event occurs when the user presses over the user interface element.

onmousemove	script	Optional. This event occurs when the user moves over the user interface element.
onmouseout	script	Optional. This event occurs when the user moves away from the user interface element.
onmouseover	script	Optional. This event occurs when the user moves over the user interface element.
onmouseup	script	Optional. This event occurs when the user releases the button over the user interface element.
standby	text	Optional. This attribute specifies a message that a user agent may render while loading the object's data.
style	style_definition	Optional. Specifies style information for the current element.
tabindex	number	Optional. Specifies the position of the current element in the tabbing order for the current document.
title	tooltip_text	Optional. Displays information about the specified element to which it is attached.
type	MIME_type	Optional. This attribute specifies the content type for the data specified by `data`.
usemap	URL	Optional. This attribute associates an image map with an element.
vspace	pixels	**Deprecated**. Optional. This attribute specifies the amount of white space to be inserted above and below an `IMG`, `APPLET`, or `OBJECT`.
width	pixels	Optional. Image and object width override.

See also:
`<FRAME>, <FRAMESET>, <IFRAME>, <NOFRAMES>,`

<ol>

Description:
The `ol` tag defines the start of an ordered list.

Requires closing tag:
Yes

Attributes:

NAME	VALUE	DESCRIPTION
class	class_rule or style_rule	Optional. Assigns a class name or set of class names to an element.
compact	compact_rendering	**Deprecated.** Optional. Renders the list in a compact way.
dir	ltr or rtl	Optional. Sets the text direction to LTR (*Left To Right*) or RTL (*Right To Left*).
id	id_name	Optional. This attribute assigns a name to an element. This name must be unique within the document.
lang	language_code	Optional. Specifies the base language of an element's attribute for both values and text content.
onclick	script	Optional. This event occurs when the user clicks on the user interface element.
ondblclick	script	Optional. This event occurs when the user double-clicks on the user interface element.
onkeydown	script	Optional. This event occurs when the user presses the specified key down on the user interface element.
onkeypress	script	Optional. This event occurs when the user presses and

		releases a key on the user interface element.
onkeyup	script	Optional. This event occurs when the user releases a key on the user interface element.
onmousedown	script	Optional. This event occurs when the user presses over the user interface element.
onmousemove	script	Optional. This event occurs when the user moves over the user interface element.
onmouseout	script	Optional. This event occurs when the user moves away from the user interface element.
onmouseover	script	Optional. This event occurs when the user moves over the user interface element.
onmouseup	script	Optional. This event occurs when the user releases the button over the user interface element.
start	start_on_number	**Deprecated.** Optional. This attribute specifies the starting number of the first item in an ordered list.
style	style_definition	Optional. Specifies style information for the current element.
title	tooltip_text	Optional. Displays information about the specified element to which it is attached.
type	A, a, I, i, 1	**Deprecated.** Optional. This attribute sets the style of a list item.

See also:
`<DIR>, <LI>, <MENU>, <UL>`

<optgroup>

Description:
The OPTGROUP element allows authors to group choices logically. This is particularly helpful when the user must choose from a long list of options; groups of related choices are easier to grasp and remember than a single long list of options.

Requires closing tag:
Yes

Attributes:

NAME	VALUE	DESCRIPTION
class	class_rule or style_rule	Optional. Assigns a class name or set of class names to an element.
dir	ltr or rtl	Optional. Sets the text direction to LTR (*Left To Right*) or RTL (*Right To Left*).
disabled	disabled	Optional. Disables the control of user input.
id	id_name	Optional. This attribute assigns a name to an element. This name must be unique within the document.
label	text_label	Required. This attribute allows authors to specify a shorter label for an option than the content of the OPTION element.
lang	language_code	Optional. Specifies the base language of an element's attribute for both values and text content.
onclick	script	Optional. This event occurs when the user clicks on the user interface element.
ondblclick	script	Optional. This event occurs when the user double-clicks on

		the user interface element.
onkeydown	script	Optional. This event occurs when the user presses the specified key down on the user interface element.
onkeypress	script	Optional. This event occurs when the user presses and releases a key on the user interface element.
onkeyup	script	Optional. This event occurs when the user releases a key on the user interface element.
onmousedown	script	Optional. This event occurs when the user presses over the user interface element.
onmousemove	script	Optional. This event occurs when the user moves over the user interface element.
onmouseout	script	Optional. This event occurs when the user moves away from the user interface element.
onmouseover	script	Optional. This event occurs when the user moves over the user interface element.
onmouseup	script	Optional. This event occurs when the user releases the button over the user interface element.
style	style_definition	Optional. Specifies style information for the current element.
title	tooltip_text	Optional. Displays information about the specified element to which it is attached.

See also:
`<OPTION>, <SELECT>`

<option>

Description:
The `option` element defines an `option` in the drop-down list.

Requires closing tag:
Yes

Attributes:

NAME	VALUE	DESCRIPTION
class	class_rule or style_rule	Optional. Assigns a class name or set of class names to an element.
dir	ltr or rtl	Optional. Sets the text direction to LTR (*Left To Right*) or RTL (*Right To Left*).
disabled	disabled	Optional. Disables the control of user input.
id	id_name	Optional. This attribute assigns a name to an element. This name must be unique within the document.
label	text	Required. This attribute allows authors to specify a shorter label for an option than the content of the `OPTION` element.
lang	language_code	Optional. Specifies the base language of an element's attribute for both values and text content.
onclick	script	Optional. This event occurs when the user clicks on the user interface element.
ondblclick	script	Optional. This event occurs when the user double-clicks on the user interface element.
onkeydown	script	Optional. This event occurs

		when the user presses the specified key down on the user interface element.
onkeypress	script	Optional. This event occurs when the user presses and releases a key on the user interface element.
onkeyup	script	Optional. This event occurs when the user releases a key on the user interface element.
onmousedown	script	Optional. This event occurs when the user presses over the user interface element.
onmousemove	script	Optional. This event occurs when the user moves over the user interface element.
onmouseout	script	Optional. This event occurs when the user moves away from the user interface element.
onmouseover	script	Optional. This event occurs when the user moves over the user interface element.
onmouseup	script	Optional. This event occurs when the user releases the button over the user interface element.
selected	selected	Optional. Specifies that this particular option is pre-selected.
style	style_definition	Optional. Specifies style information for the current element.
title	tooltip_text	Optional. Displays information about the specified element to which it is attached.
value	text	Optional. This attribute specifies the initial value of the control.

See also:
`<OPTGROUP>, <SELECT>`

<p>

Description:
The p tag defines the start of a paragraph.

Requires closing tag:
No

Attributes:

NAME	VALUE	DESCRIPTION
align	left, right, center, justify	**Deprecated.** Optional. This attribute specifies the horizontal alignment of its element with respect to the surrounding content.
class	class_rule or style_rule	Optional. Assigns a class name or set of class names to an element.
dir	ltr or rtl	Optional. Sets the text direction to LTR (*Left To Right*) or RTL (*Right To Left*).
id	id_name	Optional. This attribute assigns a name to an element. This name must be unique within the document.
lang	language_code	Optional. Specifies the base language of an element's attribute for both values and text content.
onclick	script	Optional. This event occurs when the user clicks on the user interface element.
ondblclick	script	Optional. This event occurs when the user double-clicks on the user interface element.
onkeydown	script	Optional. This event occurs when the user presses the specified key down on the user

		interface element.
onkeypress	script	Optional. This event occurs when the user presses and releases a key on the user interface element.
onkeyup	script	Optional. This event occurs when the user releases a key on the user interface element.
onmousedown	script	Optional. This event occurs when the user presses over the user interface element.
onmousemove	script	Optional. This event occurs when the user moves over the user interface element.
onmouseout	script	Optional. This event occurs when the user moves away from the user interface element.
onmouseover	script	Optional. This event occurs when the user moves over the user interface element.
onmouseup	script	Optional. This event occurs when the user releases the button over the user interface element.
style	style_definition	Optional. Specifies style information for the current element.
title	tooltip_text	Optional. Displays information about the specified element to which it is attached.

<param>

Description:
The param element allows you to specify the run-time settings for an object inserted into XHTML documents. `PARAM` elements specify a set of values that may be required by an object at run-time. Any number of `PARAM` elements may appear in the content of an `OBJECT` or `APPLET` element, in any order, but must be placed at the start of the content of the enclosing `OBJECT` or `APPLET` element.

Requires closing tag:
No

Attributes:

NAME	VALUE	DESCRIPTION
name	unique_name	Required. This attribute defines the name of a run-time parameter, assumed to be known by the inserted object.
type	MIME type	Optional. This attribute specifies the content type of the resource designated by the `value` attribute **only** in the case where `valuetype` is set to "ref".
value	value	Optional. This attribute specifies the value of a run-time parameter specified by `name`. Property values have no meaning to HTML; their meaning is determined by the object in question.
valuetype	data, ref, object	Optional. This attribute specifies the type of the `value` attribute.

See also:
`<APPLET>, <OBJECT>`

<pre>

Description:
The `PRE` element tells visual user agents that the enclosed text is "preformatted". The text enclosed in the pre element usually preserves spaces and line breaks. The text renders in a fixed-pitch font.

Requires closing tag:
Yes

Attributes:

NAME	VALUE	DESCRIPTION
class	class_rule or style_rule	Optional. Assigns a class name or set of class names to an element.
dir	ltr or rtl	Optional. Sets the text direction to LTR (*Left To Right*) or RTL (*Right To Left*).
id	id_name	Optional. This attribute assigns a name to an element. This name must be unique within the document.
lang	language_code	Optional. Specifies the base language of an element's attribute for both values and text content.
onclick	script	Optional. This event occurs when the user clicks on the user interface element.
ondblclick	script	Optional. This event occurs when the user double-clicks on the user interface element.
onkeydown	script	Optional. This event occurs when the user presses the specified key down on the user interface element.
onkeypress	script	Optional. This event occurs when the user presses and releases a key on the user

		interface element.
onkeyup	script	Optional. This event occurs when the user releases a key on the user interface element.
onmousedown	script	Optional. This event occurs when the user presses over the user interface element.
onmousemove	script	Optional. This event occurs when the user moves over the user interface element.
onmouseout	script	Optional. This event occurs when the user moves away from the user interface element.
onmouseover	script	Optional. This event occurs when the user moves over the user interface element.
onmouseup	script	Optional. This event occurs when the user releases the button over the user interface element.
style	style_definition	Optional. Specifies style information for the current element.
title	tooltip_text	Optional. Displays information about the specified element to which it is attached.
width	number	**Deprecated.** Optional. Sets the width of the formatted block.

<q>

Description:
This element designate quoted text.Q is intended for short quotations (inline content) that don't require paragraph breaks.

Requires closing tag:
Yes

Attributes:

NAME	VALUE	DESCRIPTION
cite	citation	Optional. This attribute is intended to give information about the source from which the quotation was borrowed.
class	class_rule or style_rule	Optional. Assigns a class name or set of class names to an element.
dir	ltr or rtl	Optional. Sets the text direction to LTR (*Left To Right*) or RTL (*Right To Left*).
id	id_name	Optional. This attribute assigns a name to an element. This name must be unique within the document.
lang	language_code	Optional. Specifies the base language of an element's attribute for both values and text content.
onclick	script	Optional. This event occurs when the user clicks on the user interface element.
ondblclick	script	Optional. This event occurs when the user double-clicks on the user interface element.
onkeydown	script	Optional. This event occurs when the user presses the specified key down on the user

		interface element.
onkeypress	script	Optional. This event occurs when the user presses and releases a key on the user interface element.
onkeyup	script	Optional. This event occurs when the user releases a key on the user interface element.
onmousedown	script	Optional. This event occurs when the user presses over the user interface element.
onmousemove	script	Optional. This event occurs when the user moves over the user interface element.
onmouseout	script	Optional. This event occurs when the user moves away from the user interface element.
onmouseover	script	Optional. This event occurs when the user moves over the user interface element.
onmouseup	script	Optional. This event occurs when the user releases the button over the user interface element.
style	style_definition	Optional. Specifies style information for the current element.
title	tooltip_text	Optional. Displays information about the specified element to which it is attached.

See also:
`<BLOCKQUOTE>`

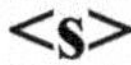

<s>

Description:
Deprecated. The `s` and `strike` tags render strike-through style text.

Requires closing tag:
Yes

Attributes:

NAME	VALUE	DESCRIPTION
class	class_rule or style_rule	Optional. Assigns a class name or set of class names to an element.
dir	ltr or rtl	Optional. Sets the text direction to LTR (*Left To Right*) or RTL (*Right To Left*).
id	id_name	Optional. This attribute assigns a name to an element. This name must be unique within the document.
lang	language_code	Optional. Specifies the base language of an element's attribute for both values and text content.
onclick	script	Optional. This event occurs when the user clicks on the user interface element.
ondblclick	script	Optional. This event occurs when the user double-clicks on the user interface element.
onkeydown	script	Optional. This event occurs when the user presses the specified key down on the user interface element.
onkeypress	script	Optional. This event occurs when the user presses and releases a key on the user interface element.

onkeyup	script	Optional. This event occurs when the user releases a key on the user interface element.
onmousedown	script	Optional. This event occurs when the user presses over the user interface element.
onmousemove	script	Optional. This event occurs when the user moves over the user interface element.
onmouseout	script	Optional. This event occurs when the user moves away from the user interface element.
onmouseover	script	Optional. This event occurs when the user moves over the user interface element.
onmouseup	script	Optional. This event occurs when the user releases the button over the user interface element.
style	style_definition	Optional. Specifies style information for the current element.
title	tooltip_text	Optional. Displays information about the specified element to which it is attached.

See also:
`<B>, <BIG>, <I>, <SMALL>, <STRIKE>, <TT>, <U>`

<samp>

Description:
Designates sample output from programs, scripts, etc.

Requires closing tag:
Yes

Attributes:

NAME	VALUE	DESCRIPTION
class	class_rule or style_rule	Optional. Assigns a class name or set of class names to an element.
dir	ltr or rtl	Optional. Sets the text direction to LTR (*Left To Right*) or RTL (*Right To Left*).
id	id_name	Optional. This attribute assigns a name to an element. This name must be unique within the document.
lang	language_code	Optional. Specifies the base language of an element's attribute for both values and text content.
onclick	script	Optional. This event occurs when the user clicks on the user interface element.
ondblclick	script	Optional. This event occurs when the user double-clicks on the user interface element.
onkeydown	script	Optional. This event occurs when the user presses the specified key down on the user interface element.
onkeypress	script	Optional. This event occurs when the user presses and releases a key on the user interface element.

onkeyup	script	Optional. This event occurs when the user releases a key on the user interface element.
onmousedown	script	Optional. This event occurs when the user presses over the user interface element.
onmousemove	script	Optional. This event occurs when the user moves over the user interface element.
onmouseout	script	Optional. This event occurs when the user moves away from the user interface element.
onmouseover	script	Optional. This event occurs when the user moves over the user interface element.
onmouseup	script	Optional. This event occurs when the user releases the button over the user interface element.
style	style_definition	Optional. Specifies style information for the current element.
title	tooltip_text	Optional. Displays information about the specified element to which it is attached.

See also:
`<ABBR>, <ACRONYM>, <CITE>, <CODE>, <DFN>, <EM>, <KBD>, <STRONG>, <VAR>`

<script>

Description:
The SCRIPT element places a script within a document. This element may appear any number of times in the HEAD or BODY of an HTML document.

Requires closing tag:
Yes

Attributes:

NAME	VALUE	DESCRIPTION
charset	charset	Optional. This attribute specifies the character encoding of the resource designated by the link.
defer	defer	Optional. Sets or retrieves the status of the script.
language	javascript, livescript, vbscript,	**Deprecated.** Optional. This attribute specifies the scripting language of the contents of this element.
src	URL	Optional. This attribute specifies the location of an external script.
type	text/ecmascript, text/javascript, application/ecmascript, application/javascript, text/vbscript	Required. This attribute specifies the scripting language of the element's contents and overrides the default scripting language.

See also:
<NOSCRIPT>

<select>

Description:
The `SELECT` element creates a menu. Each choice offered by the menu is represented by an `OPTION` element. A `SELECT` element must contain at least one `OPTION` element.

Requires closing tag:
Yes

Attributes:

NAME	VALUE	DESCRIPTION
class	class_rule or style_rule	Optional. Assigns a class name or set of class names to an element.
dir	ltr or rtl	Optional. Sets the text direction to LTR (*Left To Right*) or RTL (*Right To Left*).
disabled	disabled	Optional. Disables the control of user input.
id	id_name	Optional. This attribute assigns a name to an element. This name must be unique within the document.
lang	language_code	Optional. Specifies the base language of an element's attribute for both values and text content.
multiple	multiple	Optional. When set, this attribute allows for multiple selections.
name	unique_name	Optional. This attribute assigns the control name.
onclick	script	Optional. This event occurs when the user clicks on the user interface element.
ondblclick	script	Optional. This event occurs when the user double-clicks on the user interface element.

onkeydown	script	Optional. This event occurs when the user presses the specified key down on the user interface element.
onkeypress	script	Optional. This event occurs when the user presses and releases a key on the user interface element.
onkeyup	script	Optional. This event occurs when the user releases a key on the user interface element.
onmousedown	script	Optional. This event occurs when the user presses over the user interface element.
onmousemove	script	Optional. This event occurs when the user moves over the user interface element.
onmouseout	script	Optional. This event occurs when the user moves away from the user interface element.
onmouseover	script	Optional. This event occurs when the user moves over the user interface element.
onmouseup	script	Optional. This event occurs when the user releases the button over the user interface element.
size	number	Optional. If a `SELECT` element is presented as a scrolled list box, this attribute specifies the number of rows in the list that should be visible at the same time.
style	style_definition	Optional. Specifies style information for the current element.
tabindex	number	Optional. Specifies the position of the current element in the tabbing order for the current document.
title	tooltip_text	Optional. Displays information about the specified element to which it is attached.

See also:

`<OPTGROUP>, <OPTION>`

<small>

Description:
This element renders text in a "small" font.

Requires closing tag:
Yes

Attributes:

NAME	VALUE	DESCRIPTION
class	class_rule or style_rule	Optional. Assigns a class name or set of class names to an element.
dir	ltr or rtl	Optional. Sets the text direction to LTR (*Left To Right*) or RTL (*Right To Left*).
id	id_name	Optional. This attribute assigns a name to an element. This name must be unique within the document.
lang	language_code	Optional. Specifies the base language of an element's attribute for both values and text content.
onclick	script	Optional. This event occurs when the user clicks on the user interface element.
ondblclick	script	Optional. This event occurs when the user double-clicks on the user interface element.
onkeydown	script	Optional. This event occurs when the user presses the specified key down on the user interface element.
onkeypress	script	Optional. This event occurs when the user presses and releases a key on the user interface element.

onkeyup	script	Optional. This event occurs when the user releases a key on the user interface element.
onmousedown	script	Optional. This event occurs when the user presses over the user interface element.
onmousemove	script	Optional. This event occurs when the user moves over the user interface element.
onmouseout	script	Optional. This event occurs when the user moves away from the user interface element.
onmouseover	script	Optional. This event occurs when the user moves over the user interface element.
onmouseup	script	Optional. This event occurs when the user releases the button over the user interface element.
style	style_definition	Optional. Specifies style information for the current element.
title	tooltip_text	Optional. Displays information about the specified element to which it is attached.

See also:
`<B>, <BIG>, <I>, <S>, <STRIKE>, <TT>, <U>`

<span>

Description:
The `DIV` and `SPAN` elements, in conjunction with the `id` and `class` attributes, offer a generic mechanism for adding structure to documents. These elements define content to be inline (`SPAN`) or block-level (`DIV`) but impose no other presentational idioms on the content.

Requires closing tag:
Yes

Attributes:

NAME	VALUE	DESCRIPTION
class	class_rule or style_rule	Optional. Assigns a class name or set of class names to an element.
dir	ltr or rtl	Optional. Sets the text direction to LTR (*Left To Right*) or RTL (*Right To Left*).
id	id_name	Optional. This attribute assigns a name to an element. This name must be unique within the document.
lang	language_code	Optional. Specifies the base language of an element's attribute for both values and text content.
onclick	script	Optional. This event occurs when the user clicks on the user interface element.
ondblclick	script	Optional. This event occurs when the user double-clicks on the user interface element.
onkeydown	script	Optional. This event occurs when the user presses the specified key down on the user interface element.
onkeypress	script	Optional. This event occurs when the user presses and

		releases a key on the user interface element.
onkeyup	script	Optional. This event occurs when the user releases a key on the user interface element.
onmousedown	script	Optional. This event occurs when the user presses over the user interface element.
onmousemove	script	Optional. This event occurs when the user moves over the user interface element.
onmouseout	script	Optional. This event occurs when the user moves away from the user interface element.
onmouseover	script	Optional. This event occurs when the user moves over the user interface element.
onmouseup	script	Optional. This event occurs when the user releases the button over the user interface element.
style	style_definition	Optional. Specifies style information for the current element.
title	tooltip_text	Optional. Displays information about the specified element to which it is attached.

See also:
`<DIV>`

<strike>

Description:
Deprecated. The `s` and `strike` tags render strike-through style text.

Requires closing tag:
Yes

Attributes:

NAME	VALUE	DESCRIPTION
class	class_rule or style_rule	Optional. Assigns a class name or set of class names to an element.
dir	ltr or rtl	Optional. Sets the text direction to LTR (*Left To Right*) or RTL (*Right To Left*).
id	id_name	Optional. This attribute assigns a name to an element. This name must be unique within the document.
lang	language_code	Optional. Specifies the base language of an element's attribute for both values and text content.
onclick	script	Optional. This event occurs when the user clicks on the user interface element.
ondblclick	script	Optional. This event occurs when the user double-clicks on the user interface element.
onkeydown	script	Optional. This event occurs when the user presses the specified key down on the user interface element.
onkeypress	script	Optional. This event occurs when the user presses and releases a key on the user interface element.

onkeyup	script	Optional. This event occurs when the user releases a key on the user interface element.
onmousedown	script	Optional. This event occurs when the user presses over the user interface element.
onmousemove	script	Optional. This event occurs when the user moves over the user interface element.
onmouseout	script	Optional. This event occurs when the user moves away from the user interface element.
onmouseover	script	Optional. This event occurs when the user moves over the user interface element.
onmouseup	script	Optional. This event occurs when the user releases the button over the user interface element.
style	style_definition	Optional. Specifies style information for the current element.
title	tooltip_text	Optional. Displays information about the specified element to which it is attached.

See also:
`<B>, <BIG>, <I>, <S>, <SMALL>, <TT>, <U>`

<strong>

Description:
This attributes indicates a stronger emphasis than EM.

Requires closing tag:
Yes

Attributes:

NAME	VALUE	DESCRIPTION
class	class_rule or style_rule	Optional. Assigns a class name or set of class names to an element.
dir	ltr or rtl	Optional. Sets the text direction to LTR (*Left To Right*) or RTL (*Right To Left*).
id	id_name	Optional. This attribute assigns a name to an element. This name must be unique within the document.
lang	language_code	Optional. Specifies the base language of an element's attribute for both values and text content.
onclick	script	Optional. This event occurs when the user clicks on the user interface element.
ondblclick	script	Optional. This event occurs when the user double-clicks on the user interface element.
onkeydown	script	Optional. This event occurs when the user presses the specified key down on the user interface element.
onkeypress	script	Optional. This event occurs when the user presses and releases a key on the user interface element.

onkeyup	script	Optional. This event occurs when the user releases a key on the user interface element.
onmousedown	script	Optional. This event occurs when the user presses over the user interface element.
onmousemove	script	Optional. This event occurs when the user moves over the user interface element.
onmouseout	script	Optional. This event occurs when the user moves away from the user interface element.
onmouseover	script	Optional. This event occurs when the user moves over the user interface element.
onmouseup	script	Optional. This event occurs when the user releases the button over the user interface element.
style	style_definition	Optional. Specifies style information for the current element.
title	tooltip_text	Optional. Displays information about the specified element to which it is attached.

See also:
`<ABBR>, <ACRONYM>, <CITE>, <CODE>, <DFN>, <EM>, <KBD>, <SAMP>, <VAR>`

<style>

Description:
The STYLE element allows authors to put style sheet rules in the head of the document. HTML permits any number of STYLE elements in the HEAD section of a document.

Requires closing tag:
Yes

Attributes:

NAME	VALUE	DESCRIPTION
dir	ltr or rtl	Optional. Sets the text direction to LTR (*Left To Right*) or RTL (*Right To Left*).
lang	language_code	Optional. Specifies the base language of an element's attribute for both values and text content.
media	screen, tty, tv, projection, handheld, print, braille, aural, all	OptionalSpecifies the intended destination medium for style information.
type	text/css	Required. Specifies the style sheet language of the element's contents and will override the default style sheet language.

<sub>

Description:
The `sub` element defines text as subscript.

Requires closing tag:
Yes

Attributes:

NAME	VALUE	DESCRIPTION
class	class_rule or style_rule	Optional. Assigns a class name or set of class names to an element.
dir	ltr or rtl	Optional. Sets the text direction to LTR (*Left To Right*) or RTL (*Right To Left*).
id	id_name	Optional. This attribute assigns a name to an element. This name must be unique within the document.
lang	language_code	Optional. Specifies the base language of an element's attribute for both values and text content.
onclick	script	Optional. This event occurs when the user clicks on the user interface element.
ondblclick	script	Optional. This event occurs when the user double-clicks on the user interface element.
onkeydown	script	Optional. This event occurs when the user presses the specified key down on the user interface element.
onkeypress	script	Optional. This event occurs when the user presses and releases a key on the user interface element.

onkeyup	script	Optional. This event occurs when the user releases a key on the user interface element.
onmousedown	script	Optional. This event occurs when the user presses over the user interface element.
onmousemove	script	Optional. This event occurs when the user moves over the user interface element.
onmouseout	script	Optional. This event occurs when the user moves away from the user interface element.
onmouseover	script	Optional. This event occurs when the user moves over the user interface element.
onmouseup	script	Optional. This event occurs when the user releases the button over the user interface element.
style	style_definition	Optional. Specifies style information for the current element.
title	tooltip_text	Optional. Displays information about the specified element to which it is attached.

See also:
`<SUP>`

<sup>

Description:
The `sup` element defines text as superscript.

Requires closing tag:
Yes

Attributes:

NAME	VALUE	DESCRIPTION
class	class_rule or style_rule	Optional. Assigns a class name or set of class names to an element.
dir	ltr or rtl	Optional. Sets the text direction to LTR (*Left To Right*) or RTL (*Right To Left*).
id	id_name	Optional. This attribute assigns a name to an element. This name must be unique within the document.
lang	language_code	Optional. Specifies the base language of an element's attribute for both values and text content.
onclick	script	Optional. This event occurs when the user clicks on the user interface element.
ondblclick	script	Optional. This event occurs when the user double-clicks on the user interface element.
onkeydown	script	Optional. This event occurs when the user presses the specified key down on the user interface element.
onkeypress	script	Optional. This event occurs when the user presses and releases a key on the user interface element.

onkeyup	script	Optional. This event occurs when the user releases a key on the user interface element.
onmousedown	script	Optional. This event occurs when the user presses over the user interface element.
onmousemove	script	Optional. This event occurs when the user moves over the user interface element.
onmouseout	script	Optional. This event occurs when the user moves away from the user interface element.
onmouseover	script	Optional. This event occurs when the user moves over the user interface element.
onmouseup	script	Optional. This event occurs when the user releases the button over the user interface element.
style	style_definition	Optional. Specifies style information for the current element.
title	tooltip_text	Optional. Displays information about the specified element to which it is attached.

See also:
`<SUB>`

<table>

Description:
The HTML table model allows authors to arrange data -- text, preformatted text, images, links, forms, form fields, other tables, etc. -- into rows and columns of cells.

Requires closing tag:
Yes

Attributes:

NAME	VALUE	DESCRIPTION
align	left, center, right	**Deprecated.** Optional. Specifies the position of the table with respect to the document.
bgcolor	rgb(x,x,x), #xxxxxx, colorname	**Deprecated.** Optional. Sthe background color for the document body or table cells.
border	pixels	Optional. This attributes specifies the width (in pixels only) of the frame around a table.
cellpadding	pixels, %	Optional. This attribute specifies the amount of space between the border of the cell and its contents.
cellspacing	pixels, %	Optional. Sets the amount of space between cells.
class	class_rule or style_rule	Optional. Assigns a class name or set of class names to an element.
dir	ltr or rtl	Optional. Sets the text direction to LTR (*Left To Right*) or RTL (*Right To Left*).
frame	void, above, below, hsides, lhs, rhs, vsides, box, border	Optional. This attribute specifies which sides of the frame surrounding a table will be visible.

id	id_name	Optional. This attribute assigns a name to an element. This name must be unique within the document.
lang	language_code	Optional. Specifies the base language of an element's attribute for both values and text content.
onclick	script	Optional. This event occurs when the user clicks on the user interface element.
ondblclick	script	Optional. This event occurs when the user double-clicks on the user interface element.
onkeydown	script	Optional. This event occurs when the user presses the specified key down on the user interface element.
onkeypress	script	Optional. This event occurs when the user presses and releases a key on the user interface element.
onkeyup	script	Optional. This event occurs when the user releases a key on the user interface element.
onmousedown	script	Optional. This event occurs when the user presses over the user interface element.
onmousemove	script	Optional. This event occurs when the user moves over the user interface element.
onmouseout	script	Optional. This event occurs when the user moves away from the user interface element.
onmouseover	script	Optional. This event occurs when the user moves over the user interface element.
onmouseup	script	Optional. This event occurs when the user releases the button over the user interface element.
rules	none, groups, rows, cols, all	Optional. This attribute specifies which rules will appear between cells within a table.
style	style_definition	Optional. Specifies style

		information for the current element.
summary	text	Optional. This attribute provides a summary of the table's purpose and structure for user agents rendering to non-visual media such as speech and Braille.
title	tooltip_text	Optional. Displays information about the specified element to which it is attached.
width	%, pixels	Optional. This attribute specifies the desired width of the entire table and is intended for visual user agents.

See also:
`<CAPTION>, <COL>, <COLGROUP>, <TBODY>, <TD>, <TFOOT>, <TH>, <THEAD>, <TR>`

<tbody>

Description:
The TBODY start tag is always required except when the table contains only one table body and no table head or foot sections. The TBODY end tag may always be safely omitted.

Requires closing tag:
No

Attributes:

NAME	VALUE	DESCRIPTION
align	right, left, center, justify, char	Optional. This attribute specifies the alignment of data and the justification of text in a cell.
char	character	Optional. This attribute specifies a single character within a text fragment to act as an axis for alignment.
charoff	pixels, %	Optional. This attribute specifies the offset to the first occurrence of the alignment character on each line.
class	class_rule or style_rule	Optional. Assigns a class name or set of class names to an element.
dir	ltr or rtl	Optional. Sets the text direction to LTR (*Left To Right*) or RTL (*Right To Left*).
id	id_name	Optional. This attribute assigns a name to an element. This name must be unique within the document.
lang	language_code	Optional. Specifies the base language of an element's attribute for both values and text content.
onclick	script	Optional. This event occurs

		when the user clicks on the user interface element.
ondblclick	script	Optional. This event occurs when the user double-clicks on the user interface element.
onkeydown	script	Optional. This event occurs when the user presses the specified key down on the user interface element.
onkeypress	script	Optional. This event occurs when the user presses and releases a key on the user interface element.
onkeyup	script	Optional. This event occurs when the user releases a key on the user interface element.
onmousedown	script	Optional. This event occurs when the user presses over the user interface element.
onmousemove	script	Optional. This event occurs when the user moves over the user interface element.
onmouseout	script	Optional. This event occurs when the user moves away from the user interface element.
onmouseover	script	Optional. This event occurs when the user moves over the user interface element.
onmouseup	script	Optional. This event occurs when the user releases the button over the user interface element.
style	style_definition	Optional. Specifies style information for the current element.
title	tooltip_text	Optional. Displays information about the specified element to which it is attached.
valign	top, middle, bottom, baseline	Optional. This attribute specifies the vertical alignment of data and text in a cell.

See also:
<CAPTION>, <COL>, <COLGROUP>, <TABLE>, <TD>, <TFOOT>, <TH>, <THEAD>, <TR>

<td>

Description:
The TD element defines a cell that contains data.

Requires closing tag:
Yes

Attributes:

NAME	VALUE	DESCRIPTION
abbr	abbr_text	Optional. This attribute should be used to provide an abbreviated form of the cell's content, and may be rendered by user agents when appropriate in place of the cell's content.
align	left, right, center, justify, char	Optional. This attribute specifies the alignment of data and the justification of text in a cell.
bgcolor	rgb(x,x,x), #xxxxxx, colorname	**Deprecated.** Optional. Sets the background color for the document body or table cells.
char	character	Optional. This attribute specifies a single character within a text fragment to act as an axis for alignment.
charoff	pixels, %	Optional. This attribute specifies the offset to the first occurrence of the alignment character on each line.
class	class_rule or style_rule	Optional. Assigns a class name or set of class names to an element.
colspan	number	Optional. This attribute specifies the number of columns spanned by the current cell.

dir	ltr or rtl	Optional. Sets the text direction to LTR (*Left To Right*) or RTL (*Right To Left*).
headers	header_cells'_id	Optional. This attribute specifies the list of header cells that provide header information for the current data cell.
height	pixels	**Deprecated.** Optional. Sets a recommended cell height.
id	id_name	Optional. This attribute assigns a name to an element. This name must be unique within the document.
lang	language_code	Optional. Specifies the base language of an element's attribute for both values and text content.
nowrap	nowrap	**Deprecated.** Optional. Disables automatic text wrapping for the specified cell.
onclick	script	Optional. This event occurs when the user clicks on the user interface element.
ondblclick	script	Optional. This event occurs when the user double-clicks on the user interface element.
onkeydown	script	Optional. This event occurs when the user presses the specified key down on the user interface element.
onkeypress	script	Optional. This event occurs when the user presses and releases a key on the user interface element.
onkeyup	script	Optional. This event occurs when the user releases a key on the user interface element.
onmousedown	script	Optional. This event occurs when the user presses over the user interface element.
onmousemove	script	Optional. This event occurs when the user moves over the user interface element.
onmouseout	script	Optional. This event occurs when the user moves away from the user interface element.

onmouseover	script	Optional. This event occurs when the user moves over the user interface element.
onmouseup	script	Optional. This event occurs when the user releases the button over the user interface element.
rowspan	number	Optional. This attribute specifies the number of rows spanned by the current cell.
scope	col, colgroup, row, rowgroup	Optional. Sets the relationship of the cell to the table header.
style	style_definition	Optional. Specifies style information for the current element.
title	tooltip_text	Optional. Displays information about the specified element to which it is attached.
valign	top, middle, bottom, baseline	Optional. This attribute specifies the alignment of data and placement of text in a cell.
width	pixels, %	**Deprecated.** Optional. This attribute supplies user agents with a recommended cell width.

See also:
`<CAPTION>, <COL>, <COLGROUP>, <TABLE>, <TBODY>, <TFOOT>, <TH>, <THEAD>, <TR>`

<textarea>

Description:
The `textarea` element defines a text-area that allows users to input text in a form element.

Requires closing tag:
Yes

Attributes:

NAME	VALUE	DESCRIPTION
accesskey	character	Optional. Allows the user to use keyboard keys for functions instead of a mouse.
class	class_rule or style_rule	Optional. Assigns a class name or set of class names to an element.
cols	number	Required. This attribute specifies the number of columns.
dir	ltr or rtl	Optional. Sets the text direction to LTR (*Left To Right*) or RTL (*Right To Left*).
disabled	disabled	Optional. Disables the control of user input.
id	id_name	Optional. This attribute assigns a name to an element. This name must be unique within the document.
lang	language_code	Optional. Specifies the base language of an element's attribute for both values and text content.
name	name_of_textarea	Optional. This attribute assigns the control name.
onclick	script	Optional. This event occurs when the user clicks on the user interface element.
ondblclick	script	Optional. This event occurs

		when the user double-clicks on the user interface element.
onkeydown	script	Optional. This event occurs when the user presses the specified key down on the user interface element.
onkeypress	script	Optional. This event occurs when the user presses and releases a key on the user interface element.
onkeyup	script	Optional. This event occurs when the user releases a key on the user interface element.
onmousedown	script	Optional. This event occurs when the user presses over the user interface element.
onmousemove	script	Optional. This event occurs when the user moves over the user interface element.
onmouseout	script	Optional. This event occurs when the user moves away from the user interface element.
onmouseover	script	Optional. This event occurs when the user moves over the user interface element.
onmouseup	script	Optional. This event occurs when the user releases the button over the user interface element.
readonly	readonly	Optional. Disables changes made to the form.
rows	number	Required. Specifies the number of visible text lines.
style	style_definition	Optional. Specifies style information for the current element.
tabindex	number	Optional. Specifies the position of the current element in the tabbing order for the current document.
title	tooltip_text	Optional. Displays information about the specified element to which it is attached.

See also:

`<FIELDSET>, <FORM>, <INPUT>, <LABEL>, <LEGEND>`

<tfoot>

Description:
Table rows may be grouped into a table head, table foot, and one or more table body sections, using the `THEAD`, `TFOOT` and `TBODY` elements, respectively. This division enables user agents to support scrolling of table bodies independently of the table head and foot. When long tables are printed, the table head and foot information may be repeated on each page that contains table data.

Requires closing tag:
Yes

Attributes:

NAME	VALUE	DESCRIPTION
align	right, left, center, justify, char	Optional. This attribute specifies the alignment of data and the justification of text in a cell.
char	character	Optional. This attribute specifies a single character within a text fragment to act as an axis for alignment.
charoff	pixels, %	Optional. This attribute specifies the offset to the first occurrence of the alignment character on each line.
class	class_rule or style_rule	Optional. Assigns a class name or set of class names to an element.
dir	ltr or rtl	Optional. Sets the text direction to LTR (*Left To Right*) or RTL (*Right To Left*).
id	id_name	Optional. This attribute assigns a name to an element. This name must be unique within the document.
lang	language_code	Optional. Specifies the base language of an element's attribute for both values and

		text content.
onclick	script	Optional. This event occurs when the user clicks on the user interface element.
ondblclick	script	Optional. This event occurs when the user double-clicks on the user interface element.
onkeydown	script	Optional. This event occurs when the user presses the specified key down on the user interface element.
onkeypress	script	Optional. This event occurs when the user presses and releases a key on the user interface element.
onkeyup	script	Optional. This event occurs when the user releases a key on the user interface element.
onmousedown	script	Optional. This event occurs when the user presses over the user interface element.
onmousemove	script	Optional. This event occurs when the user moves over the user interface element.
onmouseout	script	Optional. This event occurs when the user moves away from the user interface element.
onmouseover	script	Optional. This event occurs when the user moves over the user interface element.
onmouseup	script	Optional. This event occurs when the user releases the button over the user interface element.
style	style_definition	Optional. Specifies style information for the current element.
title	tooltip_text	Optional. Displays information about the specified element to which it is attached.
valign	top, middle, bottom, baseline	Optional. This attribute specifies the alignment of data and the justification of text in a cell.

See also:
`<CAPTION>, <COL>, <COLGROUP>, <TABLE>, <TBODY>, <TD>, <TH>, <THEAD>, <TR>`

<th>

Description:
The `th` element defines a table header cell in a table. The text within the `th` element is rendered in bold.

Requires closing tag:
Yes

Attributes:

NAME	VALUE	DESCRIPTION
abbr	abbr_text	Optional. This attribute is used to provide an abbreviated form of the cell's content.
align	left, right, center, justify, char	Optional. This attribute specifies the alignment of data and the justification of text in a cell.
axis	category_names	Optional. This attribute may be used to place a cell into conceptual categories that can be considered to form axes in an n-dimensional space.
bgcolor	rgb(x,x,x), #xxxxxx, colorname	**Deprecated.** Optional. This attribute sets the background color for the document body or table cells.
char	character	Optional. This attribute specifies a single character within a text fragment to act as an axis for alignment.
charoff	pixels, %	Optional. This attribute specifies the offset to the first occurrence of the alignment character on each line.
class	class_rule or style_rule	Optional. Assigns a class name or set of class names to an element.
colspan	number	Optional. This attribute

		specifies the number of columns spanned by the current cell.
dir	ltr or rtl	Optional. Sets the text direction to LTR (*Left To Right*) or RTL (*Right To Left*).
headers	header_cells'_id	Optional. This attribute specifies the list of header cells that provide header information for the current data cell.
height	pixels	**Deprecated.** Optional. This attribute supplies user agents with a recommended cell height.
id	id_name	Optional. This attribute assigns a name to an element. This name must be unique within the document.
lang	language_code	Optional. Specifies the base language of an element's attribute for both values and text content.
nowrap	nowrap	**Deprecated.** Optional. Disables automatic text wrapping for the specific cell.
onclick	script	Optional. This event occurs when the user clicks on the user interface element.
ondblclick	script	Optional. This event occurs when the user double-clicks on the user interface element.
onkeydown	script	Optional. This event occurs when the user presses the specified key down on the user interface element.
onkeypress	script	Optional. This event occurs when the user presses and releases a key on the user interface element.
onkeyup	script	Optional. This event occurs when the user releases a key on the user interface element.
onmousedown	script	Optional. This event occurs when the user presses over the user interface element.
onmousemove	script	Optional. This event occurs

		when the user moves over the user interface element.
onmouseout	script	Optional. This event occurs when the user moves away from the user interface element.
onmouseover	script	Optional. This event occurs when the user moves over the user interface element.
onmouseup	script	Optional. This event occurs when the user releases the button over the user interface element.
rowspan	number	Optional. This attribute specifies the number of rows spanned by the current cell.
scope	col, colgroup, row, rowgroup	Optional. Specifies the set of data cells for which the current header cell provides header information.
style	style_definition	Optional. Specifies style information for the current element.
title	tooltip_text	Optional. Displays information about the specified element to which it is attached.
valign	top, middle, bottom, baseline	Optional. This attribute specifies the alignment of data and the placement of text in a cell.
width	pixels, %	**Deprecated.** Optional. This attribute sets the width of the cell.

See also:
`<CAPTION>, <COL>, <COLGROUP>, <TABLE>, <TBODY>, <TD>, <TFOOT>, <THEAD>, <TR>`

<thead>

Description:
Table rows may be grouped into a table head, table foot, and one or more table body sections, using the THEAD, TFOOT and TBODY elements, respectively. This division enables user agents to support scrolling of table bodies independently of the table head and foot. When long tables are printed, the table head and foot information may be repeated on each page that contains table data.

Requires closing tag:
Yes

Attributes:

NAME	VALUE	DESCRIPTION
align	right, left, center, justify, char	Optional. This attribute specifies the alignment of data and the justification of text in a cell.
char	character	Optional. This attribute specifies a single character within a text fragment to act as an axis for alignment.
charoff	pixels, %	Optional. This attribute specifies the offset to the first occurrence of the alignment character on each line.
class	class_rule or style_rule	Optional. Assigns a class name or set of class names to an element.
dir	ltr or rtl	Optional. Sets the text direction to LTR (*Left To Right*) or RTL (*Right To Left*).
id	id_name	Optional. This attribute assigns a name to an element. This name must be unique within the document.
lang	language_code	Optional. Specifies the base language of an element's attribute for both values and

		text content.
onclick	script	Optional. This event occurs when the user clicks on the user interface element.
ondblclick	script	Optional. This event occurs when the user double-clicks on the user interface element.
onkeydown	script	Optional. This event occurs when the user presses the specified key down on the user interface element.
onkeypress	script	Optional. This event occurs when the user presses and releases a key on the user interface element.
onkeyup	script	Optional. This event occurs when the user releases a key on the user interface element.
onmousedown	script	Optional. This event occurs when the user presses over the user interface element.
onmousemove	script	Optional. This event occurs when the user moves over the user interface element.
onmouseout	script	Optional. This event occurs when the user moves away from the user interface element.
onmouseover	script	Optional. This event occurs when the user moves over the user interface element.
onmouseup	script	Optional. This event occurs when the user releases the button over the user interface element.
style	style_definition	Optional. Specifies style information for the current element.
title	tooltip_text	Optional. Displays information about the specified element to which it is attached.
valign	top, middle, bottom, baseline	Optional. This attribute specifies the alignment of data and the justification of text in a cell.

See also:
`<CAPTION>`, `<COL>`, `<COLGROUP>`, `<TABLE>`, `<TBODY>`, `<TD>`, `<TFOOT>`, `<TH>`, `<TR>`

<title>

Description:
Authors should use the `TITLE` element to identify the contents of a document. Since users often consult documents out of context, authors should provide context-rich titles. Thus, instead of a title such as "Introduction", which doesn't provide much contextual background, authors should supply a title such as "Introduction to Medieval Bee-Keeping" instead.

Requires closing tag:
Yes

Attributes:

NAME	VALUE	DESCRIPTION
dir	ltr or rtl	Optional. Sets the text direction to LTR (*Left To Right*) or RTL (*Right To Left*).
lang	language_code	Optional. Specifies the base language of an element's attribute for both values and text content.

See also:
`<BODY>, <HEAD>, <HTML>, <META>,`

<tr>

Description:
The TR element acts as a container for a row of table cells.

Requires closing tag:
No

Attributes:

NAME	VALUE	DESCRIPTION
align	right, left, center, justify, char	Optional. This attribute specifies the alignment of data and the justification of text in a cell.
bgcolor	rgb(x,x,x), #xxxxxx, colorname	**Deprecated.** Optional. Sets the background color for the table cells.
char	character	Optional. This attribute specifies a single character within a text fragment to act as an axis for alignment.
charoff	pixels, %	Optional. This attribute specifies the offset to the first occurrence of the alignment character on each line.
class	class_rule or style_rule	Optional. Assigns a class name or set of class names to an element.
dir	ltr or rtl	Optional. Sets the text direction to LTR (*Left To Right*) or RTL (*Right To Left*).
id	id_name	Optional. This attribute assigns a name to an element. This name must be unique within the document.
lang	language_code	Optional. Specifies the base language of an element's attribute for both values and

		text content.
onclick	script	Optional. This event occurs when the user clicks on the user interface element.
ondblclick	script	Optional. This event occurs when the user double-clicks on the user interface element.
onkeydown	script	Optional. This event occurs when the user presses the specified key down on the user interface element.
onkeypress	script	Optional. This event occurs when the user presses and releases a key on the user interface element.
onkeyup	script	Optional. This event occurs when the user releases a key on the user interface element.
onmousedown	script	Optional. This event occurs when the user presses over the user interface element.
onmousemove	script	Optional. This event occurs when the user moves over the user interface element.
onmouseout	script	Optional. This event occurs when the user moves away from the user interface element.
onmouseover	script	Optional. This event occurs when the user moves over the user interface element.
onmouseup	script	Optional. This event occurs when the user releases the button over the user interface element.
style	style_definition	Optional. Specifies style information for the current element.
title	tooltip_text	Optional. Displays information about the specified element to which it is attached.
valign	top, middle, bottom, baseline	Optional. This attribute specifies the alignment of data and the text in a cell.

See also:

<CAPTION>, <COL>, <COLGROUP>, <TABLE>, <TBODY>, <TD>, <TFOOT>, <TH>, <THEAD>,

<tt>

Description:
This element renders as teletype or monospaced text.

Requires closing tag:
Yes

Attributes:

NAME	VALUE	DESCRIPTION
class	class_rule or style_rule	Optional. Assigns a class name or set of class names to an element.
dir	ltr or rtl	Optional. Sets the text direction to LTR (*Left To Right*) or RTL (*Right To Left*).
id	id_name	Optional. This attribute assigns a name to an element. This name must be unique within the document.
lang	language_code	Optional. Specifies the base language of an element's attribute for both values and text content.
onclick	script	Optional. This event occurs when the user clicks on the user interface element.
ondblclick	script	Optional. This event occurs when the user double-clicks on the user interface element.
onkeydown	script	Optional. This event occurs when the user presses the specified key down on the user interface element.
onkeypress	script	Optional. This event occurs when the user presses and releases a key on the user interface element.

onkeyup	script	Optional. This event occurs when the user releases a key on the user interface element.
onmousedown	script	Optional. This event occurs when the user presses over the user interface element.
onmousemove	script	Optional. This event occurs when the user moves over the user interface element.
onmouseout	script	Optional. This event occurs when the user moves away from the user interface element.
onmouseover	script	Optional. This event occurs when the user moves over the user interface element.
onmouseup	script	Optional. This event occurs when the user releases the button over the user interface element.
style	style_definition	Optional. Specifies style information for the current element.
title	tooltip_text	Optional. Displays information about the specified element to which it is attached.

See also:

`<B>, <BIG>, <I>, <S>, <SMALL>, <STRIKE>, <U>`

<u>

Description:
Deprecated. This element renders underlined text.

Requires closing tag:
Yes

Attributes:

NAME	VALUE	DESCRIPTION
class	class_rule or style_rule	Optional. Assigns a class name or set of class names to an element.
dir	ltr or rtl	Optional. Sets the text direction to LTR (*Left To Right*) or RTL (*Right To Left*).
id	id_name	Optional. This attribute assigns a name to an element. This name must be unique within the document.
lang	language_code	Optional. Specifies the base language of an element's attribute for both values and text content.
onclick	script	Optional. This event occurs when the user clicks on the user interface element.
ondblclick	script	Optional. This event occurs when the user double-clicks on the user interface element.
onkeydown	script	Optional. This event occurs when the user presses the specified key down on the user interface element.
onkeypress	script	Optional. This event occurs when the user presses and releases a key on the user interface element.

onkeyup	script	Optional. This event occurs when the user releases a key on the user interface element.
onmousedown	script	Optional. This event occurs when the user presses over the user interface element.
onmousemove	script	Optional. This event occurs when the user moves over the user interface element.
onmouseout	script	Optional. This event occurs when the user moves away from the user interface element.
onmouseover	script	Optional. This event occurs when the user moves over the user interface element.
onmouseup	script	Optional. This event occurs when the user releases the button over the user interface element.
style	style_definition	Optional. Specifies style information for the current element.
title	tooltip_text	Optional. Displays information about the specified element to which it is attached.

See also:

`<B>, <BIG>, <I>, <S>, <SMALL>, <STRIKE>, <TT>`

<ul>

Description:
The `ul` tag defines the start of an unordered list.

Requires closing tag:
Yes

Attributes:

NAME	VALUE	DESCRIPTION
class	class_rule or style_rule	Optional. Assigns a class name or set of class names to an element.
compact	compact_rendering	**Deprecated.** Optional. Renders the list in a more compact way.
dir	ltr or rtl	Optional. Sets the text direction to LTR (*Left To Right*) or RTL (*Right To Left*).
id	id_name	Optional. This attribute assigns a name to an element. This name must be unique within the document.
lang	language_code	Optional. Specifies the base language of an element's attribute for both values and text content.
onclick	script	Optional. This event occurs when the user clicks on the user interface element.
ondblclick	script	Optional. This event occurs when the user double-clicks on the user interface element.
onkeydown	script	Optional. This event occurs when the user presses the specified key down on the user interface element.
onkeypress	script	Optional. This event occurs when the user presses and

		releases a key on the user interface element.
onkeyup	script	Optional. This event occurs when the user releases a key on the user interface element.
onmousedown	script	Optional. This event occurs when the user presses over the user interface element.
onmousemove	script	Optional. This event occurs when the user moves over the user interface element.
onmouseout	script	Optional. This event occurs when the user moves away from the user interface element.
onmouseover	script	Optional. This event occurs when the user moves over the user interface element.
onmouseup	script	Optional. This event occurs when the user releases the button over the user interface element.
style	style_definition	Optional. Specifies style information for the current element.
title	tooltip_text	Optional. Displays information about the specified element to which it is attached.
type	disc, square, circle	**Deprecated.** Optional. This attribute sets the style of a list item.

See also:
`<DIR>, <LI>, <MENU>, <OL>`

<var>

Description:
The `var` element indicates an instance of a variable or program argument.

Requires closing tag:
Yes

Attributes:

NAME	VALUE	DESCRIPTION
class	class_rule or style_rule	Optional. Assigns a class name or set of class names to an element.
dir	ltr or rtl	Optional. Sets the text direction to LTR (*Left To Right*) or RTL (*Right To Left*).
id	id_name	Optional. This attribute assigns a name to an element. This name must be unique within the document.
lang	language_code	Optional. Specifies the base language of an element's attribute for both values and text content.
onclick	script	Optional. This event occurs when the user clicks on the user interface element.
ondblclick	script	Optional. This event occurs when the user double-clicks on the user interface element.
onkeydown	script	Optional. This event occurs when the user presses the specified key down on the user interface element.
onkeypress	script	Optional. This event occurs when the user presses and releases a key on the user interface element.

onkeyup	script	Optional. This event occurs when the user releases a key on the user interface element.
onmousedown	script	Optional. This event occurs when the user presses over the user interface element.
onmousemove	script	Optional. This event occurs when the user moves over the user interface element.
onmouseout	script	Optional. This event occurs when the user moves away from the user interface element.
onmouseover	script	Optional. This event occurs when the user moves over the user interface element.
onmouseup	script	Optional. This event occurs when the user releases the button over the user interface element.
style	style_definition	Optional. Specifies style information for the current element.
title	tooltip_text	Optional. Displays information about the specified element to which it is attached.

See also:
`<ABBR>, <ACRONYM>, <CITE>, <CODE>, <DFN>, <EM>, <KBD>, <SAMP>, <STRONG>`

CSS Properties

@charset CSS 2.0

Browser Version:

IE	FireFox	Netscape
5.5		6.0

Description:
Allows an author to specify the character set encoding of the style sheet; it should only be used on external style sheets.

Type:
@Rules

See also:
@fontdef, @font-face, @import, @media, @namespace, @page

@fontdef CSS 2.0

Browser Version:

IE	FireFox	Netscape
-		4.0

Description:
Links a font definition file to a document.

Type:
@Rules

See also:
@charset, @font-face, @import, @media, @namespace, @page

@font-face CSS 2.0

Browser Version:

IE	FireFox	Netscape
4.0		-

Description:
Maps an embedded OpenType file to a font already on the user's system or an entirely new font name.

Type:
@Rules

See also:
@charset, @fontdef, @import, @media, @namespace, @page

@import CSS 2.0

Browser Version:

IE	FireFox	Netscape
4.0		6.0

Description:
Imports a style sheet fragment file to the current style sheet. It may be used in External and Embedded style sheets, but not with inline styles.

Type:
@Rules

See also:
@charset, @fontdef, @font-face, @media, @namespace, @page

@media CSS 2.0

Browser Version:

IE	FireFox	Netscape
4.0		6.0

Description:
With this syntax, different CSS rules can be specified and applied from the same style sheet depending on whether the rendering device is the printed page, a computer screen, speech synthesizer, etc.

Type:
@Rules

See also:
@charset, @fontdef, @font-face, @import, @namespace, @page

@namespace CSS 2.0

Browser Version:

IE	FireFox	Netscape
-		6.0

Description:
This rule allows the declaration of a namespace prefix to be used by selectors in a stylesheet.

Type:
@Rules

See also:
@charset, @fontdef, @font-face, @import, @media, @page

@page CSS 2.0

Browser Version:

IE	FireFox	Netscape
5.5		-

Description:
Creates a special rectangular area where content is rendered in paged media.

Type:
@Rules

See also:
@charset, @fontdef, @font-face, @import, @media, @namespace

:active CSS 1.0

Browser Version:

IE	FireFox	Netscape
4	1	8

Description:
Adds special style to an activated element

Type:
Pseudo-Class

See also:
:canvas, :empty, :first, :first-child, :first-node, :focus, :hover, :lang, :last-child, :last-node, :left, :link, :not, :right, :root, :scrolled-content, :viewport, :viewport-scroll, :visited

:after

CSS 2.0

Browser Version:

IE	FireFox	Netscape
-	1.5	8

Description:
Inserts some content after an element

Type:
Pseudo-Element

See also:
:before, :first-letter, :first-line

:before CSS 2.0

Browser Version:

IE	FireFox	Netscape
-	1.5	8

Description:
Inserts some content before an element

Type:
Pseudo-Element

See also:
:after, :first-letter, :first-line

:canvas CSS 2.0

Browser Version:

IE	FireFox	Netscape
6.0		

Description:
Indicates a virtual component of a document - the rendering canvas.

Type:
Pseudo-Class

See also:
:active, :empty, :first, :first-child, :first-node, :focus, :hover, :lang, :last-child, :last-node, :left, :link, :not, :right, :root, :scrolled-content, :viewport, :viewport-scroll, :visited

:empty CSS 2.0

Browser Version:

IE	FireFox	Netscape
6.0		

Description:
Applied to elements or contexts that have no content. An element is considered to have content if it is a container element, and has at least one or more text or other elements inside it.

Type:
Pseudo-Class

See also:
:active, :canvas, :first, :first-child, :first-node, :focus, :hover, :lang, :last-child, :last-node, :left, :link, :not, :right, :root, :scrolled-content, :viewport, :viewport-scroll, :visited

:first CSS 2.0

Browser Version:

IE	FireFox	Netscape
-		-

Description:
Only applied with the @Page rule used to define styles for Page Boxes. All printed pages will automatically be classified as either a :left or :right.

Type:
Pseudo-Class

See also:
:active, :canvas, :empty, :first-child, :first-node, :focus, :hover, :lang, :last-child, :last-node, :left, :link, :not, :right, :root, :scrolled-content, :viewport, :viewport-scroll, :visited

:first-child

CSS 2.0

Browser Version:

IE	FireFox	Netscape
-	1	7

Description:
Adds special style to an element that is the first child of some other element

Type:
Pseudo-Class

See also:
:active, :canvas, :empty, :first, :first-node, :focus, :hover, :lang, :last-child, :last-node, :left, :link, :not, :right, :root, :scrolled-content, :viewport, :viewport-scroll, :visited

:first-letter CSS 1.0

Browser Version:

IE	FireFox	Netscape
5	1	8

Description:
Adds special style to the first letter of a text

Type:
Pseudo-Element

See also:
:after, :before, :first-line

:first-line CSS 1.0

Browser Version:

IE	FireFox	Netscape
5	1	8

Description:
Adds special style to the first line of a text

Type:
Pseudo-Element

See also:
:after, :before, :first-letter

:first-node CSS 2.0

Browser Version:

IE	FireFox	Netscape
-		6.0

Description:
Selects the first occurrence of an element in the document tree.

Type:
Pseudo-Class

See also:
:active, :canvas, :empty, :first, :first-child, :focus, :hover, :lang, :last-child, :last-node, :left, :link, :not, :right, :root, :scrolled-content, :viewport, :viewport-scroll, :visited

:focus CSS 2.0

Browser Version:

IE	FireFox	Netscape
-	1.5	8

Description:
Adds special style to an element while the element has focus

Type:
Pseudo-Class

See also:
:active, :canvas, :empty, :first, :first-child, :first-node, :hover, :lang, :last-child, :last-node, :left, :link, :not, :right, :root, :scrolled-content, :viewport, :viewport-scroll, :visited

:hover CSS 1.0

Browser Version:

IE	FireFox	Netscape
4	1	7

Description:
Adds special style to an element when you mouse over it

Type:
Pseudo-Class

See also:
:active, :canvas, :empty, :first, :first-child, :first-node, :focus, :lang, :last-child, :last-node, :left, :link, :not, :right, :root, :scrolled-content, :viewport, :viewport-scroll, :visited

:lang CSS 2.0

Browser Version:

IE	FireFox	Netscape
-	1	8

Description:
Allows the author to specify a language to use in a specified element

Type:
Pseudo-Class

See also:
:active, :canvas, :empty, :first, :first-child, :first-node, :focus, :hover, :last-child, :last-node, :left, :link, :not, :right, :root, :scrolled-content, :viewport, :viewport-scroll, :visited

:last-child CSS 2.0

Browser Version:

IE	FireFox	Netscape
-	-	6.0

Description:
Selects an element context that is the last child node of another selector in the document element tree.

Type:
Pseudo-Classes

See also:
:active, :canvas, :empty, :first, :first-child, :first-node, :focus, :hover, :lang, :last-node, :left, :link, :not, :right, :root, :scrolled-content, :viewport, :viewport-scroll, :visited

:last-node CSS 2.0

Browser Version:

IE	FireFox	Netscape
-		6.0

Description:
Selects the last occurrence of an element in the document tree.

Type:
Pseudo-Class

See also:
:active, :canvas, :empty, :first, :first-child, :first-node, :focus, :hover, :lang, :last-child, :left, :link, :not, :right, :root, :scrolled-content, :viewport, :viewport-scroll, :visited

:left CSS 2.0

Browser Version:

IE	FireFox	Netscape
-		6.0

Description:
Only applied with the @Page rule used to define styles for Page Boxes.

Type:
Pseudo-Class

See also:
:active, :canvas, :empty, :first, :first-child, :first-node, :focus, :hover, :lang, :last-child, :last-node, :link, :not, :right, :root, :scrolled-content, :viewport, :viewport-scroll, :visited

:link CSS 1.0

Browser Version:

IE	FireFox	Netscape
3	1	4

Description:
Adds special style to an unvisited link

Type:
Pseudo-Class

See also:
:active, :canvas, :empty, :first, :first-child, :first-node, :focus, :hover, :lang, :last-child, :last-node, :left, :not, :right, :root, :scrolled-content, :viewport, :viewport-scroll, :visited

:not CSS 2.0

Browser Version:

IE	FireFox	Netscape
-		6.0

Description:
Used to negate a normal selector; CSS selectors are used to narrow down the set of elements that a rule set will apply to. The *:not* pseudo-class directs the CSS to apply a rule set to everything that you did *NOT* select.

Type:
Pseudo-Class

See also:
:active, :canvas, :empty, :first, :first-child, :first-node, :focus, :hover, :lang, :last-child, :last-node, :left, :link, :right, :root, :scrolled-content, :viewport, :viewport-scroll, :visited

:right CSS 2.0

Browser Version:

IE	FireFox	Netscape
-		6.0

Description:
Only applied with the @Page rule used to define styles for Page Boxes.

Type:
Pseudo-Class

See also:
:active, :canvas, :empty, :first, :first-child, :first-node, :focus, :hover, :lang, :last-child, :last-node, :left, :link, :not, :root, :scrolled-content, :viewport, :viewport-scroll, :visited

:root CSS 2.0

Browser Version:

IE	FireFox	Netscape
-		6.0

Description:
Calculates from the document tree - it indicates the top-level of a document.

Type:
Pseudo-Class

See also:
:active, :canvas, :empty, :first, :first-child, :first-node, :focus, :hover, :lang, :last-child, :last-node, :left, :link, :not, :right, :scrolled-content, :viewport, :viewport-scroll, :visited

:scrolled-content CSS 2.0

Browser Version:

IE	FireFox	Netscape
-		6.0

Description:
Applies to content that is scrolled in a visual rendering environment.

Type:
Pseudo-Class

See also:
:active, :canvas, :empty, :first, :first-child, :first-node, :focus, :hover, :lang, :last-child, :last-node, :left, :link, :not, :right, :root, :viewport, :viewport-scroll, :visited

:viewport CSS 2.0

Browser Version:

IE	FireFox	Netscape
-		6.0

Description:
Indicates a virtual piece of a document - the rendering viewport.

Type:
Pseudo-Class

See also:
:active, :canvas, :empty, :first, :first-child, :first-node, :focus, :hover, :lang, :last-child, :last-node, :left, :link, :not, :right, :root, :scrolled-content, :viewport-scroll, :visited

:viewport-scroll CSS 2.0

Browser Version:

IE	FireFox	Netscape
-		6.0

Description:
Indicates a virtual component of a document - the rendering viewport,

Type:
Pseudo-Class

See also:
:active, :canvas, :empty, :first, :first-child, :first-node, :focus, :hover, :lang, :last-child, :last-node, :left, :link, :not, :right, :root, :scrolled-content, :viewport, :visited

:visited CSS 1.0

Browser Version:

IE	FireFox	Netscape
3	1	4

Description:
Adds special style to a visited link

Type:
Pseudo-Class

See also:
:active, :canvas, :empty, :first, :first-child, :first-node, :focus, :hover, :lang, :last-child, :last-node, :left, :link, :not, :right, :root, :scrolled-content, :viewport, :viewport-scroll

accelerator CSS 2.0

Browser Version:

IE	FireFox	Netscape
5.0	-	-

Description:
A Microsoft specific property that has the ability to turn off its system underlines for accelerator keys until the ALT key is pressed.

Value:
false
true

Type:
Dynamic Content

See also:
behavior, cursor, filter, zoom

azimuth CSS 2.0

Browser Version:

IE	FireFox	Netscape

Description:
Sets where the sound/voices should come from (horizontally)

Value:
angle
left-side
far-left
left
center-left
center
center-right
right
far-right
right-side
behind
leftwards
rightwards

Type:
Aural

See also:
cue, cue-after, cue-before, elevation, pause, pause-after, pause-before, pitch, pitch-range, play-during, richness, speak, speak-numeral, speak-punctuation, speech-rate, stress, voice-family, volume

background CSS 1.0

Browser Version:

IE	FireFox	Netscape
4	1	6

Description:
A shorthand property for setting all background properties in one declaration

Value:
background-color
background-image
background-repeat background-attachment background-position

Type:
Backgrounds

See also:
background-attachment, background-color, background-image, background-position, background-position-x, background-position-y, background-repeat, color, layer-background-color, layer-background-image

background-attachment CSS 1.0

Browser Version:

IE	FireFox	Netscape
4	1	6

Description:
Sets whether a background image is fixed or scrolls with the rest of the page

Value:
scroll
fixed

Type:
Backgrounds

See also:
background, background-color, background-image, background-position, background-position-x, background-position-y, background-repeat, color, layer-background-color, layer-background-image

background-color CSS 1.0

Browser Version:

IE	FireFox	Netscape
4	1	4

Description:
Sets the background color of an element

Value:
color-rgb
color-hex
color-name
transparent

Type:
Backgrounds

See also:
background, background-attachment, background-image, background-position, background-position-x, background-position-y, background-repeat, color, layer-background-color, layer-background-image

background-image CSS 1.0

Browser Version:

IE	FireFox	Netscape
4	1	4

Description:
Sets an image as the background

Value:
url
none

Type:
Backgrounds

See also:
background, background-attachment, background-color, background-position, background-position-x, background-position-y, background-repeat, color, layer-background-color, layer-background-image

background-position CSS 1.0

Browser Version:

IE	FireFox	Netscape
4	1	6

Description:
Sets the starting position of a background image

Value:
top left
top center
top right
center left
center center
center right
bottom left
bottom center
bottom right
x% y%
xpos ypos

Type:
Backgrounds

See also:
background, background-attachment, background-color, background-image, background-position-x, background-position-y, background-repeat, color, layer-background-color, layer-background-image

background-position-x CSS 2.0

Browser Version:

IE	FireFox	Netscape
5.5	-	-

Description:
Specifies the initial position on the X-axis of the background image specified in the browser window.

Value:
center
left
length
percentage
right

Type:
Backgrounds

See also:
background, background-attachment, background-color, background-image, background-position, background-position-y, background-repeat, color, layer-background-color, layer-background-image

background-position-y CSS 2.0

Browser Version:

IE	FireFox	Netscape
5.5	-	-

Description:
Specifies the initial position on the Y-axis of the background image specified in the browser window.

Value:
center
left
length
percentage
right

Type:
Backgrounds

See also:
background, background-attachment, background-color, background-image, background-position, background-position-x, background-repeat, color, layer-background-color, layer-background-image

background-repeat CSS 1.0

Browser Version:

IE	FireFox	Netscape
4	1	4

Description:
Sets if/how a background image will be repeated

Value:
repeat
repeat-x
repeat-y
no-repeat

Type:
Backgrounds

See also:
background, background-attachment, background-color, background-image, background-position, background-position-x, background-position-y, color, layer-background-color, layer-background-image

behavior CSS 2.0

Browser Version:

IE	FireFox	Netscape
5.0	-	-

Description:
Specifies one or more space separated URLs indicating scripts to attach to a CSS selector.

Value:
#Object ID
default behavior
script url

Type:
Dynamic Content

See also:
accelerator, cursor, filter, zoom

border CSS 1.0

Browser Version:

IE	FireFox	Netscape
4	1	4

Description:
A shorthand property for setting all of the properties for the four borders in one declaration

Value:
border-width
border-style
border-color

Type:
Borders

See also:
border-bottom, border-bottom-color, border-bottom-style, border-bottom-width, border-color, border-left, border-left-color, border-left-style, border-left-width, border-right, border-right-color, border-right-style, border-right-width, border-style, border-top, border-top-color, border-top-style, border-top-width, border-width

border-bottom CSS 1.0

Browser Version:

IE	FireFox	Netscape
4	1	6

Description:
A shorthand property for setting all of the properties for the bottom border in one declaration

Value:
border-bottom-width
border-style
border-color

Type:
Borders

See also:
border, border-bottom-color, border-bottom-style, border-bottom-width, border-color, border-left, border-left-color, border-left-style, border-left-width, border-right, border-right-color, border-right-style, border-right-width, border-style, border-top, border-top-color, border-top-style, border-top-width, border-width

border-bottom-color CSS 2.0

Browser Version:

IE	FireFox	Netscape
4	1	6

Description:
Sets the color of the bottom border

Value:
border-color

Type:
Borders

See also:
border, border-bottom, border-bottom-style, border-bottom-width, border-color, border-left, border-left-color, border-left-style, border-left-width, border-right, border-right-color, border-right-style, border-right-width, border-style, border-top, border-top-color, border-top-style, border-top-width, border-width

border-bottom-style CSS 2.0

Browser Version:

IE	FireFox	Netscape
4	1	6

Description:
Sets the style of the bottom border

Value:
border-style

Type:
Borders

See also:
border, border-bottom, border-bottom-color, border-bottom-width, border-color, border-left, border-left-color, border-left-style, border-left-width, border-right, border-right-color, border-right-style, border-right-width, border-style, border-top, border-top-color, border-top-style, border-top-width, border-width

border-bottom-width CSS 1.0

Browser Version:

IE	FireFox	Netscape
4	1	4

Description:
Sets the width of the bottom border

Value:
thin
medium
thick
length

Type:
Borders

See also:
border, border-bottom, border-bottom-color, border-bottom-style, border-color, border-left, border-left-color, border-left-style, border-left-width, border-right, border-right-color, border-right-style, border-right-width, border-style, border-top, border-top-color, border-top-style, border-top-width, border-width

border-collapse CSS 2.0

Browser Version:

IE	FireFox	Netscape
5	1	7

Description:
Sets whether the table borders are collapsed into a single border or detached as in standard HTML

Value:
collapse
separate

Type:
Tables

See also:
border-spacing, caption-side, empty-cells, speak-header, table-layout

border-color CSS 1.0

Browser Version:

IE	FireFox	Netscape
4	1	6

Description:
Sets the color of the four borders, can have from one to four colors

Value:
color

Type:
Borders

See also:
border, border-bottom, border-bottom-color, border-bottom-style, border-bottom-width, border-left, border-left-color, border-left-style, border-left-width, border-right, border-right-color, border-right-style, border-right-width, border-style, border-top, border-top-color, border-top-style, border-top-width, border-width

border-left CSS 1.0

Browser Version:

IE	FireFox	Netscape
4	1	6

Description:
A shorthand property for setting all of the properties for the left border in one declaration

Value:
border-left-width
border-style
border-color

Type:
Borders

See also:
border, border-bottom, border-bottom-color, border-bottom-style, border-bottom-width, border-color, border-left-color, border-left-style, border-left-width, border-right, border-right-color, border-right-style, border-right-width, border-style, border-top, border-top-color, border-top-style, border-top-width, border-width

border-left-color CSS 2.0

Browser Version:

IE	FireFox	Netscape
4	1	6

Description:
Sets the color of the left border

Value:
border-color

Type:
Borders

See also:
border, border-bottom, border-bottom-color, border-bottom-style, border-bottom-width, border-color, border-left, border-left-style, border-left-width, border-right, border-right-color, border-right-style, border-right-width, border-style, border-top, border-top-color, border-top-style, border-top-width, border-width

border-left-style CSS 2.0

Browser Version:

IE	FireFox	Netscape
4	1	6

Description:
Sets the style of the left border

Value:
border-style

Type:
Borders

See also:
border, border-bottom, border-bottom-color, border-bottom-style, border-bottom-width, border-color, border-left, border-left-color, border-left-width, border-right, border-right-color, border-right-style, border-right-width, border-style, border-top, border-top-color, border-top-style, border-top-width, border-width

border-left-width CSS 1.0

Browser Version:

IE	FireFox	Netscape
4	1	4

Description:
Sets the width of the left border

Value:
thin
medium
thick
length

Type:
Borders

See also:
border, border-bottom, border-bottom-color, border-bottom-style, border-bottom-width, border-color, border-left, border-left-color, border-left-style, border-right, border-right-color, border-right-style, border-right-width, border-style, border-top, border-top-color, border-top-style, border-top-width, border-width

border-right CSS 1.0

Browser Version:

IE	FireFox	Netscape
4	1	6

Description:
A shorthand property for setting all of the properties for the right border in one declaration

Value:
border-right-width
border-style
border-color

Type:
Borders

See also:
border, border-bottom, border-bottom-color, border-bottom-style, border-bottom-width, border-color, border-left, border-left-color, border-left-style, border-left-width, border-right-color, border-right-style, border-right-width, border-style, border-top, border-top-color, border-top-style, border-top-width, border-width

border-right-color CSS 2.0

Browser Version:

IE	FireFox	Netscape
4	1	6

Description:
Sets the color of the right border

Value:
border-color

Type:
Borders

See also:
border, border-bottom, border-bottom-color, border-bottom-style, border-bottom-width, border-color, border-left, border-left-color, border-left-style, border-left-width, border-right, border-right-style, border-right-width, border-style, border-top, border-top-color, border-top-style, border-top-width, border-width

border-right-style CSS 2.0

Browser Version:

IE	FireFox	Netscape
4	1	6

Description:
Sets the style of the right border

Value:
border-style

Type:
Borders

See also:
border, border-bottom, border-bottom-color, border-bottom-style, border-bottom-width, border-color, border-left, border-left-color, border-left-style, border-left-width, border-right, border-right-color, border-right-width, border-style, border-top, border-top-color, border-top-style, border-top-width, border-width

border-right-width CSS 1.0

Browser Version:

IE	FireFox	Netscape
4	1	4

Description:
Sets the width of the right border

Value:
thin
medium
thick
length

Type:
Borders

See also:
border, border-bottom, border-bottom-color, border-bottom-style, border-bottom-width, border-color, border-left, border-left-color, border-left-style, border-left-width, border-right, border-right-color, border-right-style, border-style, border-top, border-top-color, border-top-style, border-top-width, border-width

border-spacing CSS 2.0

Browser Version:

IE	FireFox	Netscape
5M	1	6

Description:
Sets the distance that separates cell borders (only for the \"separated borders\" model)

Value:
length

Type:
Tables

See also:
border-collapse, caption-side, empty-cells, speak-header, table-layout

border-style CSS 1.0

Browser Version:

IE	FireFox	Netscape
4	1	6

Description:
Sets the style of the four borders, can have from one to four styles

Value:
none
hidden
dotted
dashed
solid
double
groove
ridge
inset
outset

Type:
Borders

See also:
border, border-bottom, border-bottom-color, border-bottom-style, border-bottom-width, border-color, border-left, border-left-color, border-left-style, border-left-width, border-right, border-right-color, border-right-style, border-right-width, border-style, border-top, border-top-color, border-top-style, border-top-width, border-width

border-top CSS 1.0

Browser Version:

IE	FireFox	Netscape
4	1	6

Description:
A shorthand property for setting all of the properties for the top border in one declaration

Value:
border-top-width
border-style
border-color

Type:
Borders

See also:
border, border-bottom, border-bottom-color, border-bottom-style, border-bottom-width, border-color, border-left, border-left-color, border-left-style, border-left-width, border-right, border-right-color, border-right-style, border-right-width, border-style, border-top-color, border-top-style, border-top-width, border-width

border-top-color CSS 2.0

Browser Version:

IE	FireFox	Netscape
4	1	6

Description:
Sets the color of the top border

Value:
border-color

Type:
Borders

See also:
border, border-bottom, border-bottom-color, border-bottom-style, border-bottom-width, border-color, border-left, border-left-color, border-left-style, border-left-width, border-right, border-right-color, border-right-style, border-right-width, border-style, border-top, border-top-style, border-top-width, border-width

border-top-style CSS 2.0

Browser Version:

IE	FireFox	Netscape
4	1	6

Description:
Sets the style of the top border

Value:
border-style

Type:
Borders

See also:
border, border-bottom, border-bottom-color, border-bottom-style, border-bottom-width, border-color, border-left, border-left-color, border-left-style, border-left-width, border-right, border-right-color, border-right-style, border-right-width, border-style, border-top, border-top-color, border-top-width, border-width

border-top-width CSS 1.0

Browser Version:

IE	FireFox	Netscape
4	1	4

Description:
Sets the width of the top border

Value:
thin
medium
thick
length

Type:
Borders

See also:
border, border-bottom, border-bottom-color, border-bottom-style, border-bottom-width, border-color, border-left, border-left-color, border-left-style, border-left-width, border-right, border-right-color, border-right-style, border-right-width, border-style, border-top, border-top-color, border-top-style, border-width

border-width CSS 1.0

Browser Version:

IE	FireFox	Netscape
4	1	4

Description:
A shorthand property for setting the width of the four borders in one declaration, can have from one to four values

Value:
thin
medium
thick
length

Type:
Borders

See also:
border, border-bottom, border-bottom-color, border-bottom-style, border-bottom-width, border-color, border-left, border-left-color, border-left-style, border-left-width, border-right, border-right-color, border-right-style, border-right-width, border-style, border-top, border-top-color, border-top-style, border-top-width

bottom CSS 2.0

Browser Version:

IE	FireFox	Netscape
5	1	6

Description:
Sets how far the bottom edge of an element is above/below the bottom edge of the parent element

Value:
auto
%
length

Type:
Positioning

See also:
clip, left, overflow, overflow-x, overflow-y, right, text-overflow, top, vertical-align, z-index

caption-side CSS 2.0

Browser Version:

IE	FireFox	Netscape
5M	1	6

Description:
Sets the position of the table caption

Value:
top
bottom
left
right

Type:
Tables

See also:
border-collapse, border-spacing, empty-cells, speak-header, table-layout

clear CSS 1.0

Browser Version:

IE	FireFox	Netscape
4	1	4

Description:
Sets the sides of an element where other floating elements are not allowed

Value:
left
right
both
none

Type:
Classification

See also:
display, float, position, visibility

clip CSS 2.0

Browser Version:

IE	FireFox	Netscape
4	1	6

Description:
Sets the shape of an element. The element is clipped into this shape, and displayed

Value:
shape
auto

Type:
Positioning

See also:
bottom, left, overflow, overflow-x, overflow-y, right, text-overflow, top, vertical-align, z-index

color CSS 1.0

Browser Version:

IE	FireFox	Netscape
3	1	4

Description:
Sets the color of a text

Value:
color

Type:
Backgrounds

See also:
background, background-attachment, background-color, background-image, background-position, background-position-x, background-position-y, background-repeat, layer-background-color, layer-background-image

content CSS 2.0

Browser Version:

IE	FireFox	Netscape
-	1	6

Description:
Generates content in a document. Used with the :before and :after pseudo-elements

Value:
string
url
counter(name)
counter(name, list-style-type)
counters(name, string)
counters(name, string, list-style-type)
attr(X)
open-quote
close-quote
no-open-quote
no-close-quote

Type:
Generated Content

See also:
counter-increment, counter-reset, include-source, quotes

counter-increment CSS 2.0

Browser Version:

IE	FireFox	Netscape
-	-	-

Description:
Sets how much the counter increments on each occurrence of a selector

Value:
none
identifier number

Type:
Generated Content

See also:
content, counter-reset, include-source, quotes

counter-reset CSS 2.0

Browser Version:

IE	FireFox	Netscape
-	-	-

Description:
Sets the value the counter is set to on each occurrence of a selector

Value:
none
identifier number

Type:
Generated Content

See also:
content, counter-increment, counter-reset, include-source, quotes

cue CSS 2.0

Browser Version:

IE	FireFox	Netscape

Description:
A shorthand property for setting the cue-before and cue-after properties in one declaration

Value:
cue-before
cue-after

Type:
Aural

See also:
azimuth, cue-after, cue-before, elevation, pause, pause-after, pause-before, pitch, pitch-range, play-during, richness, speak, speak-numeral, speak-punctuation, speech-rate, stress, voice-family, volume

cue-after CSS 2.0

Browser Version:

IE	FireFox	Netscape

Description:
Specifies a sound to be played after speaking an element's content to delimit it from other

Value:
none
url

Type:
Aural

See also:
azimuth, cue, cue-before, elevation, pause, pause-after, pause-before, pitch, pitch-range, play-during, richness, speak, speak-numeral, speak-punctuation, speech-rate, stress, voice-family, volume

cue-before CSS 2.0

Browser Version:

IE	FireFox	Netscape

Description:
Specifies a sound to be played before speaking an element's content to delimit it from other

Value:
none
url

Type:
Aural

See also:
azimuth, cue, cue-after, elevation, pause, pause-after, pause-before, pitch, pitch-range, play-during, richness, speak, speak-numeral, speak-punctuation, speech-rate, stress, voice-family, volume

cursor CSS 2.0

Browser Version:

IE	FireFox	Netscape
4	1	6

Description:
Specifies the type of cursor to be displayed

Value:
url
auto
crosshair
default
pointer
move
e-resize
ne-resize
nw-resize
n-resize
se-resize
sw-resize
s-resize
w-resize
text
wait
help

Type:
Dynamic Content

See also:
acceleration, behavior, filter, zoom

direction CSS 2.0

Browser Version:

IE	FireFox	Netscape
6	1	6

Description:
Sets the text direction

Value:
ltr
rtl

Type:
International

See also:
ime-mode, layout-flow, layout-grid, layout-grid-char, layout-grid-char-spacing, layout-grid-line, layout-grid-type, line-break, ruby-align, ruby-overhang, ruby-position, text-autospace, text-justify, text-kashida-space, unicode-bidi, word-break, writing-mode

display CSS 1.0

Browser Version:

IE	FireFox	Netscape
4	1	4

Description:
Sets how/if an element is displayed

Value:
none
inline
block
list-item
run-in
compact
marker
table
inline-table
table-row-group
table-header-group
table-footer-group
table-row
table-column-group
table-column
table-cell
table-caption

Type:
Classification

See also:
clear, float, position, visibility

elevation CSS 2.0

Browser Version:

IE	FireFox	Netscape

Description:
Sets where the sound/voices should come from (vertically)

Value:
angle
below
level
above
higher
lower

Type:
Aural

See also:
azimuth, cue, cue-after, cue-before, pause, pause-after, pause-before, pitch, pitch-range, play-during, richness, speak, speak-numeral, speak-punctuation, speech-rate, stress, voice-family, volume

empty-cells CSS 2.0

Browser Version:

IE	FireFox	Netscape
5M	1	6

Description:
Sets whether or not to show empty cells in a table (only for the \"separated borders\" model)

Value:
show
hide

Type:
Tables

See also:
border-collapse, border-spacing, caption-side, speak-header, table-layout

filter CSS 2.0

Browser Version:

IE	FireFox	Netscape
4.0	-	-

Description:
This property creates an extensible mechanism allowing special visual effects to be applied to content.

Value:
transition filters
transition filters
visual filters

Type:
Dynamic Content

See also:
accelerator, behavior, cursor, zoom

float CSS 1.0

Browser Version:

IE	FireFox	Netscape
4	1	4

Description:
Sets where an image or a text will appear in another element

Value:
left
right
none

Type:
Classification

See also:
clear, display, position, visibility

font CSS 1.0

Browser Version:

IE	FireFox	Netscape
4	1	4

Description:
A shorthand property for setting all of the properties for a font in one declaration

Value:
font-style
font-variant
font-weight
font-size/line-height
font-family
caption
icon
menu
message-box
small-caption
status-bar

Type:
Fonts

See also:
font-family, font-size, font-size-adjust, font-stretch, font-style, font-variant, font-weight

font-family CSS 1.0

Browser Version:

IE	FireFox	Netscape
3	1	4

Description:
A prioritized list of font family names and/or generic family names for an element

Value:
family-name
generic-family

Type:
Fonts

See also:
font, font-size, font-size-adjust, font-stretch, font-style, font-variant, font-weight

font-size CSS 1.0

Browser Version:

IE	FireFox	Netscape
3	1	4

Description:
Sets the size of a font

Value:
xx-small
x-small
small
medium
large
x-large
xx-large
smaller
larger
length
%

Type:
Fonts

See also:
font, font-family, font-size-adjust, font-stretch, font-style, font-variant, font-weight

font-size-adjust CSS 2.0

Browser Version:

IE	FireFox	Netscape
-	1	-

Description:
Specifies an aspect value for an element that will preserve the x-height of the first-choice font

Value:
none
number

Type:
Fonts

See also:
font, font-family, font-size, font-stretch, font-style, font-variant, font-weight

font-stretch CSS 2.0

Browser Version:

IE	FireFox	Netscape
-	-	-

Description:
Condenses or expands the current font-family

Value:
normal
wider
narrower
ultra-condensed
extra-condensed
condensed
semi-condensed
semi-expanded
expanded
extra-expanded
ultra-expanded

Type:
Fonts

See also:
font, font-family, font-size, font-size-adjust, font-style, font-variant, font-weight

font-style CSS 1.0

Browser Version:

IE	FireFox	Netscape
4	1	4

Description:
Sets the style of the font

Value:
normal
italic
oblique

Type:
Fonts

See also:
font, font-family, font-size, font-size-adjust, font-stretch, font-variant, font-weight

font-variant CSS 1.0

Browser Version:

IE	FireFox	Netscape
4	1	6

Description:
Displays text in a small-caps font or a normal font

Value:
normal
small-caps

Type:
Fonts

See also:
font, font-family, font-size, font-size-adjust, font-stretch, font-style, font-weight

font-weight CSS 1.0

Browser Version:

IE	FireFox	Netscape
4	1	4

Description:
Sets the weight of a font

Value:
normal
bold
bolder
lighter
100
200
300
400
500
600
700
800
900

Type:
Fonts

See also:
font, font-family, font-size, font-size-adjust, font-stretch, font-style, font-variant

height CSS 1.0

Browser Version:

IE	FireFox	Netscape
4	1	6

Description:
Sets the height of an element

Value:
auto
length
%

Type:
Dimensions

See also:
line-height, max-height, max-width, min-height, min-width, width

ime-mode CSS 2.0

Browser Version:

IE	FireFox	Netscape
5.0	-	-

Description:
This property controls the state of an Input Method Editor (IME) for user text entry fields.

Value:
active
auto
deactivated
inactive

Type:
International

See also:
direction, layout-flow, layout-grid, layout-grid-char, layout-grid-char-spacing, layout-grid-line, layout-grid-type, line-break, ruby-align, ruby-overhang, ruby-position, text-autospace, text-justify, text-kashida-space, unicode-bidi, word-break, writing-mode

include-source CSS 2.0

Browser Version:

IE	FireFox	Netscape
-	-	4.0

Description:
This property inserts another document into the current document, replacing the current element's content

Value:
URL

Type:
Generated Content

See also:
content, counter-increment, counter-reset, quotes

layer-background-color CSS 2.0

Browser Version:

IE	FireFox	Netscape
-	-	4.0

Description:
Sets the background-color for the entire region of the current element

Value:
color
transparent

Type:
Backgrounds

See also:
background, background-attachment, background-color, background-image, background-position, background-position-x, background-position-y, background-repeat, color, layer-background-image

layout-flow CSS 2.0

Browser Version:

IE	FireFox	Netscape
5.5	-	-

Description:
This property controls the direction and flow of the content in an element

Value:
horizontal
vertical-ideographic

Type:
International

See also:
direction, ime-mode, layout-grid, layout-grid-char, layout-grid-char-spacing, layout-grid-line, layout-grid-type, line-break, ruby-align, ruby-overhang, ruby-position, text-autospace, text-justify, text-kashida-space, unicode-bidi, word-break, writing-mode

layout-grid   CSS 2.0

Browser Version:

IE	FireFox	Netscape
5.0	-	-

Description:
This property controls the direction and flow of the content in an element.

Value:
horizontal
vertical-ideographic

Type:
International

See also:
direction, ime-mode, layout-flow, layout-grid-char, layout-grid-char-spacing, layout-grid-line, layout-grid-type, line-break, ruby-align, ruby-overhang, ruby-position, text-autospace, text-justify, text-kashida-space, unicode-bidi, word-break, writing-mode

layout-grid-char CSS 2.0

Browser Version:

IE	FireFox	Netscape
5.0	-	-

Description:
The 'layout-grid' property is a shorthand method used to set the 'layout-grid-mode', 'layout-grid-type', 'layout-grid-line', 'layout-grid-char', and 'layout-grid-char-spacing' properties using a single property notation.

Value:
layout-grid-mode
layout-grid-type
layout-grid-line
layout-grid-char
layout-grid-char-spacing

Type:
International

See also:
direction, ime-mode, layout-flow, layout-grid, layout-grid-char-spacing, layout-grid-line, layout-grid-type, line-break, ruby-align, ruby-overhang, ruby-position, text-autospace, text-justify, text-kashida-space, unicode-bidi, word-break, writing-mode

layout-grid-char-spacing

CSS 2.0

Browser Version:

IE	FireFox	Netscape
5.0	-	-

Description:
This property controls the character spacing granularity when the 'layout-grid-mode' is set to 'char' or 'both', and the 'layout-grid-type' property is set to 'loose'. Visually, this property has an effect similar to the 'line-height' property.

Value:
auto
length
percentage

Type:
International

See also:
direction, ime-mode, layout-flow, layout-grid, layout-grid-char, layout-grid-line, layout-grid-type, line-break, ruby-align, ruby-overhang, ruby-position, text-autospace, text-justify, text-kashida-space, unicode-bidi, word-break, writing-mode

layout-grid-line CSS 2.0

Browser Version:

IE	FireFox	Netscape
5.0	-	-

Description:
This property controls the grid length granularity when the 'layout-grid-mode' is set to 'line' or 'both'.

Value:
auto
length
none
percentage

Type:
International

See also:
direction, ime-mode, layout-flow, layout-grid, layout-grid-char, layout-grid-char-spacing, layout-grid-type, line-break, ruby-align, ruby-overhang, ruby-position, text-autospace, text-justify, text-kashida-space, unicode-bidi, word-break, writing-mode

layout-grid-type CSS 2.0

Browser Version:

IE	FireFox	Netscape
5.0	-	-

Description:
This property controls the type of layout grid used when rendering an element's text content.

Value:
fixed
loose
strict

Type:
International

See also:
direction, ime-mode, layout-flow, layout-grid, layout-grid-char, layout-grid-char-spacing, layout-grid-line, line-break, ruby-align, ruby-overhang, ruby-position, text-autospace, text-justify, text-kashida-space, unicode-bidi, word-break, writing-mode

left CSS 2.0

Browser Version:

IE	FireFox	Netscape
4	1	4

Description:
Sets how far the left edge of an element is to the right/left of the left edge of the parent element

Value:
auto
%
length

Type:
Positioning

See also:
bottom, clip, overflow, overflow-x, overflow-y, right, text-overflow, top, vertical-align, z-index

letter-spacing CSS 1.0

Browser Version:

IE	FireFox	Netscape
4	1	6

Description:
Increase or decrease the space between characters

Value:
normal
length

Type:
Text

See also:
text-align, text-align-last, text-decoration, text-indent, text-shadow, text-transform, text-underline-position, white-space, word-spacing, word-wrap

line-break CSS 2.0

Browser Version:

IE	FireFox	Netscape
5.0	-	-

Description:
This property controls whether or not a strict line-breaking behavior is used.

Value:
normal
strict

Type:
International

See also:
direction, ime-mode, layout-flow, layout-grid, layout-grid-char, layout-grid-char-spacing, layout-grid-line, layout-grid-type, ruby-align, ruby-overhang, ruby-position, text-autospace, text-justify, text-kashida-space, unicode-bidi, word-break, writing-mode

line-height CSS 1.0

Browser Version:

IE	FireFox	Netscape
4	1	4

Description:
Sets the distance between lines

Value:
normal
number
length
%

Type:
Dimensions

See also:
height, max-height, max-width, min-height, min-width, width

list-style CSS 1.0

Browser Version:

IE	FireFox	Netscape
4	1	6

Description:
A shorthand property for setting all of the properties for a list in one declaration

Value:
list-style-type
list-style-position
list-style-image

Type:
Lists

See also:
list-style-image, list-style-position, list-style-type, marker-offset

list-style-image CSS 1.0

Browser Version:

IE	FireFox	Netscape
4	1	6

Description:
Sets an image as the list-item marker

Value:
none
url

Type:
Lists

See also:
list-style, list-style-position, list-style-type, marker-offset

list-style-position CSS 1.0

Browser Version:

IE	FireFox	Netscape
4	1	6

Description:
Sets where the list-item marker is placed in the list

Value:
inside
outside

Type:
Lists

See also:
list-style, list-style-image, list-style-type, marker-offset

list-style-type CSS 1.0

Browser Version:

IE	FireFox	Netscape
4	1	4

Description:
Sets the type of the list-item marker

Value:
none
disc
circle
square
decimal
decimal-leading-zero
lower-roman
upper-roman
lower-alpha
upper-alpha
lower-greek
lower-latin
upper-latin
hebrew
armenian
georgian
cjk-ideographic
hiragana
katakana
hiragana-iroha
katakana-iroha

Type:
Lists

See also:

list-style, list-style-image, list-style-position, marker-offset

margin CSS 1.0

Browser Version:

IE	FireFox	Netscape
4	1	4

Description:
A shorthand property for setting the margin properties in one declaration

Value:
margin-top
margin-right
margin-bottom
margin-left

Type:
Margins

See also:
margin-bottom, margin-left, margin-right, margin-top

margin-bottom CSS 1.0

Browser Version:

IE	FireFox	Netscape
4	1	4

Description:
Sets the bottom margin of an element

Value:
auto
length
%

Type:
Margins

See also:
margin, margin-left, margin-right, margin-top

margin-left CSS 1.0

Browser Version:

IE	FireFox	Netscape
3	1	4

Description:
Sets the left margin of an element

Value:
auto
length
%

Type:
Margins

See also:
margin, margin-bottom, margin-right, margin-top

margin-right CSS 1.0

Browser Version:

IE	FireFox	Netscape
3	1	4

Description:
Sets the right margin of an element

Value:
auto
length
%

Type:
Margins

See also:
margin, margin-bottom, margin-left, margin-top

margin-top CSS 1.0

Browser Version:

IE	FireFox	Netscape
3	1	4

Description:
Sets the top margin of an element

Value:
auto
length
%

Type:
Margins

See also:
margin, margin-bottom, margin-left, margin-right

marker-offset CSS 2.0

Browser Version:

IE	FireFox	Netscape
-	1	7

Description:
This property gives a horizontal distance between the marker box and the principal rendering box, measured between the adjacent neighboring edges of the two boxes.

Value:
auto
inherit
length

Type:
Lists

See also:
list-style, list-style-image, list-style-position, list-style-type

marks CSS 2.0

Browser Version:

IE	FireFox	Netscape

Description:
Sets what sort of marks should be rendered outside the page box

Value:
none
crop
cross

Type:
Printing

See also:
orphans, page, page-break-after, page-break-before, page-break-inside, size, widows

max-height CSS 2.0

Browser Version:

IE	FireFox	Netscape
-	1	6

Description:
Sets the maximum height of an element

Value:
none
length
%

Type:
Dimensions

See also:
height, line-height, max-width, min-height, min-width, width

max-width CSS 2.0

Browser Version:

IE	FireFox	Netscape
-	1	6

Description:
Sets the maximum width of an element

Value:
none
length
%

Type:
Dimensions

See also:
height, line-height, max-height, min-height, min-width, width

min-height CSS 2.0

Browser Version:

IE	FireFox	Netscape
-	1	6

Description:
Sets the minimum height of an element

Value:
length
%

Type:
Dimensions

See also:
height, line-height, max-height, max-width, min-width, width

min-width CSS 2.0

Browser Version:

IE	FireFox	Netscape
-	1	6

Description:
Sets the minimum width of an element

Value:
length
%

Type:
Dimensions

See also:
height, line-height, max-height, max-width, min-height, width

orphans CSS 2.0

Browser Version:

IE	FireFox	Netscape

Description:
Sets the minimum number of lines for a paragraph that must be left at the bottom of a page

Value:
number

Type:
Printing

See also:
marks, page, page-break-after, page-break-before, page-break-inside, size, widows

outline CSS 2.0

Browser Version:

IE	FireFox	Netscape
-	1.5	-

Description:
A shorthand property for setting all the outline properties in one declaration

Value:
outline-color
outline-style
outline-width

Type:
Outline

See also:
outline-color, outline-style, outline-width

outline-color CSS 2.0

Browser Version:

IE	FireFox	Netscape
-	1.5	-

Description:
Sets the color of the outline around an element

Value:
color
invert

Type:
Outline

See also:
outline, outline-style, outline-width

outline-style CSS 2.0

Browser Version:

IE	FireFox	Netscape
-	1.5	-

Description:
Sets the style of the outline around an element

Value:
none
dotted
dashed
solid
double
groove
ridge
inset
outset

Type:
Outline

See also:
outline, outline-color, outline-width

outline-width CSS 2.0

Browser Version:

IE	FireFox	Netscape
-	1.5	-

Description:
Sets the width of the outline around an element

Value:
thin
medium
thick
length

Type:
Outline

See also:
outline, outline-color, outline-style

overflow CSS 2.0

Browser Version:

IE	FireFox	Netscape
4	1	6

Description:
Sets what happens if the content of an element overflow its area

Value:
visible
hidden
scroll
auto

Type:
Positioning

See also:
bottom, clip, left, overflow-x, overflow-y, right, text-overflow, top, vertical-align, z-index

overflow-x CSS 2.0

Browser Version:

IE	FireFox	Netscape
5.0	-	-

Description:
This property describes what to do with the content that exceeds the element's width.

Value:
auto
hidden
scroll
visible

Type:
Positioning

See also:
bottom, clip, left, overflow, overflow-y, right, text-overflow, top, vertical-align, z-index

overflow-y CSS 2.0

Browser Version:

IE	FireFox	Netscape
5.0	-	-

Description:
This property describes what to do with the content that exceeds the element's height.

Value:
auto
hidden
scroll
visible

Type:
Positioning

See also:
bottom, clip, left, overflow, overflow-x, right, text-overflow, top, vertical-align, z-index

padding CSS 1.0

Browser Version:

IE	FireFox	Netscape
4	1	4

Description:
A shorthand property for setting all of the padding properties in one declaration

Value:
padding-top
padding-right
padding-bottom
padding-left

Type:
Padding

See also:
padding-bottom, padding-left, padding-right, padding-top

padding-bottom CSS 1.0

Browser Version:

IE	FireFox	Netscape
4	1	4

Description:
Sets the bottom padding of an element

Value:
length
%

Type:
Padding

See also:
padding, padding-left, padding-right, padding-top

padding-left

CSS 1.0

Browser Version:

IE	FireFox	Netscape
4	1	4

Description:
Sets the left padding of an element

Value:
length
%

Type:
Padding

See also:
padding, padding-bottom, padding-right, padding-top

padding-right CSS 1.0

Browser Version:

IE	FireFox	Netscape
4	1	4

Description:
Sets the right padding of an element

Value:
length

Type:
Padding

See also:
padding, padding-bottom, padding-left, padding-top

padding-top CSS 1.0

Browser Version:

IE	FireFox	Netscape
4	1	4

Description:
Sets the top padding of an element

Value:
length
%

Type:
Padding

See also:
padding, padding-bottom, padding-left, padding-right

page CSS 2.0

Browser Version:

IE	FireFox	Netscape

Description:
Sets a page type to use when displaying an element

Value:
auto
identifier

Type:
Printing

See also:
marks, orphans, page-break-after, page-break-before, page-break-inside, size, widows

page-break-after CSS 2.0

Browser Version:

IE	FireFox	Netscape

Description:
Sets the page-breaking behavior after an element

Value:
auto
always
avoid
left
right

Type:
Printing

See also:
marks, orphans, page, page-break-before, page-break-inside, size, widows

page-breaking-before CSS 2.0

Browser Version:

IE	FireFox	Netscape

Description:
Sets the page-breaking behavior before an element

Value:
auto
always
avoid
left
right

Type:
Printing

See also:
marks, orphans, page, page-break-after, page-break-inside, size, widows

page-break-inside CSS 2.0

Browser Version:

IE	FireFox	Netscape

Description:
Sets the page-breaking behavior inside an element

Value:
auto
avoid

Type:
Printing

See also:
marks, orphans, page, page-break-after, page-break-before, size, widows

pause CSS 2.0

Browser Version:

IE	FireFox	Netscape

Description:
A shorthand property for setting the pause-before and pause-after properties in one declaration

Value:
pause-before
pause-after

Type:
Aural

See also:
azimuth, cue, cue-after, cue-before, elevation, pause-after, pause-before, pitch, pitch-range, play-during, richness, speak, speak-numeral, speak-punctuation, speech-rate, stress, voice-family, volume

pause-after CSS 2.0

Browser Version:

IE	FireFox	Netscape

Description:
Specifies a pause after speaking an element's content

Value:
time
%

Type:
Aural

See also:
zimuth, cue, cue-after, cue-before, elevation, pause, pause-before, pitch, pitch-range, play-during, richness, speak, speak-numeral, speak-punctuation, speech-rate, stress, voice-family, volume

pause-before CSS 2.0

Browser Version:

IE	FireFox	Netscape

Description:
Specifies a pause before speaking an element's content

Value:
time
%

Type:
Aural

See also:
azimuth, cue, cue-after, cue-before, elevation, pause, pause-after, pitch, pitch-range, play-during, richness, speak, speak-numeral, speak-punctuation, speech-rate, stress, voice-family, volume

pitch CSS 2.0

Browser Version:

IE	FireFox	Netscape

Description:
Specifies the speaking voice

Value:
frequency
x-low
low
medium
high
x-high

Type:
Aural

See also:
azimuth, cue, cue-after, cue-before, elevation, pause, pause-after, pause-before, pitch-range, play-during, richness, speak, speak-numeral, speak-punctuation, speech-rate, stress, voice-family, volume

pitch-range CSS 2.0

Browser Version:

IE	FireFox	Netscape

Description:
Specifies the variation in the speaking voice. (Monotone voice or animated voice)

Value:
number

Type:
Aural

See also:
azimuth, cue, cue-after, cue-before, elevation, pause, pause-after, pause-before, pitch, play-during, richness, speak, speak-numeral, speak-punctuation, speech-rate, stress, voice-family, volume

play-during CSS 2.0

Browser Version:

IE	FireFox	Netscape

Description:
Specifies a sound to be played while speaking an element's content

Value:
auto
none
url
mix
repeat

Type:
Aural

See also:
azimuth, cue, cue-after, cue-before, elevation, pause, pause-after, pause-before, pitch, pitch-range, richness, speak, speak-numeral, speak-punctuation, speech-rate, stress, voice-family, volume

position CSS 2.0

Browser Version:

IE	FireFox	Netscape
4	1	4

Description:
Places an element in a static, relative, absolute or fixed position

Value:
static
relative
absolute
fixed

Type:
Classification

See also:
clear, display, float, visibility

quotes CSS 2.0

Browser Version:

IE	FireFox	Netscape
-	1	6

Description:
Sets the type of quotation marks

Value:
none
string string

Type:
Generated Content

See also:
content, counter-increment, counter-reset, include-source

richness CSS 2.0

Browser Version:

IE	FireFox	Netscape

Description:
Specifies the richness in the speaking voice. (Rich voice or thin voice?)

Value:
number

Type:
Aural

See also:
azimuth, cue, cue-after, cue-before, elevation, pause, pause-after, pause-before, pitch, pitch-range, play-during, speak, speak-numeral, speak-punctuation, speech-rate, stress, voice-family, volume

right CSS 2.0

Browser Version:

IE	FireFox	Netscape
5	1	6

Description:
Sets how far the right edge of an element is to the left/right of the right edge of the parent element

Value:
auto
%
length

Type:
Positioning

See also:
bottom, clip, left, overflow, overflow-x, overflow-y, text-overflow, top, vertical-align, z-index

ruby-align

CSS 2.0

Browser Version:

IE	FireFox	Netscape
5.0	-	-

Description:
This property specifies the horizontal alignment of the Ruby Text (RT) relative to the RUBY element content.

Value:
auto
center
distribute-letter
distribute-space
left
line-edge
right

Type:
International

See also:
direction, ime-mode, layout-flow, layout-grid, layout-grid-char, layout-grid-char-spacing, layout-grid-line, layout-grid-type, line-break, ruby-overhang, ruby-position, text-autospace, text-justify, text-kashida-space, unicode-bidi, word-break, writing-mode

ruby-overhang CSS 2.0

Browser Version:

IE	FireFox	Netscape
5.0	-	-

Description:
This property describes how Ruby Text (RT) content will "hang" over other non-ruby content if the RT content is wider than the RUBY content.

Value:
auto
none
whitespace

Type:
International

See also:
direction, ime-mode, layout-flow, layout-grid, layout-grid-char, layout-grid-char-spacing, layout-grid-line, layout-grid-type, line-break, ruby-align, ruby-position, text-autospace, text-justify, text-kashida-space, unicode-bidi, word-break, writing-mode

ruby-position CSS 2.0

Browser Version:

IE	FireFox	Netscape
5.0	-	-

Description:
This property specifies the position of the helper Ruby Text (RT) relative to the Ruby content.

Value:
above
inline

Type:
International

See also:
direction, ime-mode, layout-flow, layout-grid, layout-grid-char, layout-grid-char-spacing, layout-grid-line, layout-grid-type, line-break, ruby-align, ruby-overhang, text-autospace, text-justify, text-kashida-space, unicode-bidi, word-break, writing-mode

scrollbar-3dlight-color CSS 2.0

Browser Version:

IE	FireFox	Netscape
5.5		-

Description:
Defines the color for the scrollbar 3dlight color.

Value:
color

Type:
Scrollbars

See also:
scrollbar-arrow-color, scrollbar-base-color, scrollbar-darkshadow-color, scrollbar-face-color, scrollbar-highlight-color, scrollbar-shadow-color, scrollbar-track-color

scrollbar-arrow-color CSS 2.0

Browser Version:

IE	FireFox	Netscape
5.5		-

Description:
Defines the color for the scrollbar arrow.

Value:
color

Type:
Scrollbars

See also:
scrollbar3dlight-color, scrollbar-base-color, scrollbar-darkshadow-color, scrollbar-face-color, scrollbar-highlight-color, scrollbar-shadow-color, scrollbar-track-color

scrollbar-base-color CSS 2.0

Browser Version:

IE	FireFox	Netscape
5.0		-

Description:
Defines the color for the scrollbar base color.

Value:
color

Type:
Scrollbars

See also:
scrollbar3dlight-color, scrollbar-arrow-color, scrollbar-darkshadow-color, scrollbar-face-color, scrollbar-highlight-color, scrollbar-shadow-color, scrollbar-track-color

scrollbar-darkshadow-color CSS 2.0

Browser Version:

IE	FireFox	Netscape
5.0		-

Description:
Defines the color for the dark shadow on the scrollbar .

Value:
color

Type:
Scrollbars

See also:
scrollbar3dlight-color, scrollbar-arrow-color, scrollbar-base-color, scrollbar-face-color, scrollbar-highlight-color, scrollbar-shadow-color, scrollbar-track-color

scrollbar-face-color CSS 2.0

Browser Version:

IE	FireFox	Netscape
5.0		-

Description:
Defines the color for the face of the scrollbar.

Value:
color

Type:
Scrollbars

See also:
scrollbar3dlight-color, scrollbar-arrow-color, scrollbar-base-color, scrollbar-darkshadow-color, scrollbar-highlight-color, scrollbar-shadow-color, scrollbar-track-color

scrollbar-highlight-color CSS 2.0

Browser Version:

IE	FireFox	Netscape
5.0		-

Description:
Defines the highlight color for the scrollbar.

Value:
color

Type:
Scrollbars

See also:
scrollbar3dlight-color, scrollbar-arrow-color, scrollbar-base-color, scrollbar-darkshadow-color, scrollbar-face-color, scrollbar-shadow-color, scrollbar-track-color

scrollbar-shadow-color CSS 2.0

Browser Version:

IE	FireFox	Netscape
5.0		-

Description:
Defines the color for the shadow of the scrollbar.

Value:
color

Type:
Scrollbars

See also:
scrollbar3dlight-color, scrollbar-arrow-color, scrollbar-base-color, scrollbar-darkshadow-color, scrollbar-face-color, scrollbar-highlight-color, scrollbar-track-color

scrollbar-track-color CSS 2.0

Browser Version:

IE	FireFox	Netscape
5.0		-

Description:
Defines the color for the scrollbar track.

Value:
color

Type:
Scrollbars

See also:
scrollbar3dlight-color, scrollbar-arrow-color, scrollbar-base-color, scrollbar-darkshadow-color, scrollbar-face-color, scrollbar-highlight-color, scrollbar-shadow-color

size CSS 2.0

Browser Version:

IE	FireFox	Netscape

Description:
Sets the orientation and size of a page

Value:
auto
portrait
landscape

Type:
Printing

See also:
marks, orphans, page, page-break-after, page-break-before, page-break-inside, widows

speak CSS 2.0

Browser Version:

IE	FireFox	Netscape

Description:
Specifies whether content will render aurally

Value:
normal
none
spell-out

Type:
Aural

See also:
azimuth, cue, cue-after, cue-before, elevation, pause, pause-after, pause-before, pitch, pitch-range, play-during, richness, speak-numeral, speak-punctuation, speech-rate, stress, voice-family, volume

speak-header CSS 2.0

Browser Version:

IE	FireFox	Netscape

Description:
Specifies how to handle table headers. Should the headers be spoken before every cell, or only before a cell with a different header than the previous cell

Value:
always
once

Type:
Tables

See also:
border-collapse, border-spacing, caption-side, empty-cells, table-layout

speak-numeral CSS 2.0

Browser Version:

IE	FireFox	Netscape

Description:
Specifies how to speak numbers

Value:
digits
continuous

Type:
Aural

See also:
azimuth, cue, cue-after, cue-before, elevation, pause, pause-after, pause-before, pitch, pitch-range, play-during, richness, speak, speak-punctuation, speech-rate, stress, voice-family, volume

speak-punctuation CSS 2.0

Browser Version:

IE	FireFox	Netscape

Description:
Specifies how to speak punctuation characters

Value:
none
code

Type:
Aural

See also:
azimuth, cue, cue-after, cue-before, elevation, pause, pause-after, pause-before, pitch, pitch-range, play-during, richness, speak, speak-numeral, speech-rate, stress, voice-family, volume

speech-rate CSS 2.0

Browser Version:

IE	FireFox	Netscape

Description:
Specifies the speed of the speaking

Value:
number
x-slow
slow
medium
fast
x-fast
faster
slower

Type:
Aural

See also:

azimuth, cue, cue-after, cue-before, elevation, pause, pause-after, pause-before, pitch, pitch-range, play-during, richness, speak, speak-numeral, speak-punctuation, stress, voice-family, volume

stress CSS 2.0

Browser Version:

IE	FireFox	Netscape

Description:
Specifies the stress in the speaking voice

Value:
number

Type:
Aural

See also:
azimuth, cue, cue-after, cue-before, elevation, pause, pause-after, pause-before, pitch, pitch-range, play-during, richness, speak, speak-numeral, speak-punctuation, speech-rate, voice-family, volume

table-layout CSS 2.0

Browser Version:

IE	FireFox	Netscape
5	1	6

Description:
Sets the algorithm used to display the table cells, rows, and columns

Value:
auto
fixed

Type:
Tables

See also:
border-collapse, border-spacing, caption-side, empty-cells, speak-header

text-align CSS 1.0

Browser Version:

IE	FireFox	Netscape
4	1	4

Description:
Aligns the text in an element

Value:
left
right
center
justify

Type:
Text

See also:
letter-spacing, text-align-last, text-decoration, text-indent, text-shadow, text-transform, text-underline-position, white-space, word-spacing, word-wrap

text-align-last

CSS 2.0

Browser Version:

IE	FireFox	Netscape
5.5	-	-

Description:
Used in conjunction with the 'text-align' property, but the value specified overrides the effects of that property on the horizontal alignment of the last or only rendered line of an element.

Value:
auto
center
inherit
justify
left
right

Type:
Text

See also:
letter-spacing, text-align, text-decoration, text-indent, text-shadow, text-transform, text-underline-position, white-space, word-spacing, word-wrap

text-autospace CSS 2.0

Browser Version:

IE	FireFox	Netscape
5.0	-	-

Description:
This property controls the autospacing and narrow space width adjustment behavior of text.

Value:
ideograph-alpha
ideograph-numeric
ideograph-parenthesis
ideograph-space
none

Type:
International

See also:
direction, ime-mode, layout-flow, layout-grid, layout-grid-char, layout-grid-char-spacing, layout-grid-line, layout-grid-type, line-break, ruby-align, ruby-overhang, ruby-position, text-justify, text-kashida-space, unicode-bidi, word-break, writing-mode

text-decoration CSS 1.0

Browser Version:

IE	FireFox	Netscape
4	1	4

Description:
Adds decoration to text

Value:
none
underline
overline
line-through
blink

Type:
Text

See also:
letter-spacing, text-align, text-align-last, text-indent, text-shadow, text-transform, text-underline-position, white-space, word-spacing, word-wrap

text-indent CSS 1.0

Browser Version:

IE	FireFox	Netscape
4	1	4

Description:
Indents the first line of text in an element

Value:
length
%

Type:
Text

See also:
letter-spacing, text-align, text-align-last, text-decoration, text-shadow, text-transform, text-underline-position, white-space, word-spacing, word-wrap

text-justify CSS 2.0

Browser Version:

IE	FireFox	Netscape
5.5	-	-

Description:
This property offers a refinement on the "justify" value used in the 'text-align' property.

Value:
auto
distribute
distribute-all-lines
inter-cluster
inter-ideograph
inter-word
newspaper

Type:
International

See also:
direction, ime-mode, layout-flow, layout-grid, layout-grid-char, layout-grid-char-spacing, layout-grid-line, layout-grid-type, line-break, ruby-align, ruby-overhang, ruby-position, text-autospace, text-kashida-space, unicode-bidi, word-break, writing-mode

text-kashida-space CSS 2.0

Browser Version:

IE	FireFox	Netscape
5.5	-	-

Description:
This property controls the ratio of kashida expansion to white-space expansion when justifying lines of text in an element.

Value:
inherit
percentage

Type:
International

See also:
direction, ime-mode, layout-flow, layout-grid, layout-grid-char, layout-grid-char-spacing, layout-grid-line, layout-grid-type, line-break, ruby-align, ruby-overhang, ruby-position, text-autospace, text-justify, unicode-bidi, word-break, writing-mode

text-overflow CSS 2.0

Browser Version:

IE	FireFox	Netscape
6.0	-	-

Description:
When content falls outside the rendering box, this property defines what content will be visible.

Value:
clip
ellipsis

Type:
Positioning

See also:
bottom, clip, left, overflow, overflow-x, overflow-y, right, top, vertical-align, z-index

text-shadow CSS 2.0

Browser Version:

IE	FireFox	Netscape
-	-	-

Description:
Ddefines one or more comma-separated shadow effects to be applied to the text content of the current element.

Value:
none
color
length

Type:
Text

See also:
letter-spacing, text-align, text-align-last, text-decoration, text-indent, text-transform, text-underline-position, white-space, word-spacing, word-wrap

text-transform

CSS 1.0

Browser Version:

IE	FireFox	Netscape
4	1	4

Description:
Controls the letters in an element

Value:
none
capitalize
uppercase
lowercase

Type:
Text

See also:
letter-spacing, text-align, text-align-last, text-decoration, text-indent, text-shadow, text-underline-position, white-space, word-spacing, word-wrap

text-underline-position CSS 2.0

Browser Version:

IE	FireFox	Netscape
5.5	-	-

Description:
Specifies the default position of the underline that is set using the 'text-decoration' property "underline" value.

Value:
above
auto
auto-pos
below

Type:
Text

See also:
letter-spacing, text-align, text-align-last, text-decoration, text-indent, text-shadow, text-transform, white-space, word-spacing, word-wrap

top CSS 2.0

Browser Version:

IE	FireFox	Netscape
4	1	4

Description:
Sets how far the top edge of an element is above/below the top edge of the parent element

Value:
auto
%
length

Type:
Positioning

See also:
bottom, clip, left, overflow, overflow-x, overflow-y, right, text-overflow, vertical-align, z-index

unicode-bidi CSS 2.0

Browser Version:

IE	FireFox	Netscape
5	-	-

Description:
Allows for a complex process of determining the directional flow of content.

Value:
normal
embed
bidi-override

Type:
International

See also:
direction, ime-mode, layout-flow, layout-grid, layout-grid-char, layout-grid-char-spacing, layout-grid-line, layout-grid-type, line-break, ruby-align, ruby-overhang, ruby-position, text-autospace, text-justify, text-kashida-space, word-break, writing-mode

vertical-align CSS 1.0

Browser Version:

IE	FireFox	Netscape
4	1	4

Description:
Sets the vertical alignment of an element

Value:
baseline
sub
super
top
text-top
middle
bottom
text-bottom
length
%

Type:
Positioning

See also:
bottom, clip, left, overflow, overflow-x, overflow-y, right, text-overflow, top, z-index

visibility CSS 2.0

Browser Version:

IE	FireFox	Netscape
4	1	6

Description:
Sets if an element should be visible or invisible

Value:
visible
hidden
collapse

Type:
Classification

See also:
clear, display, float, position

voice-family CSS 2.0

Browser Version:

IE	FireFox	Netscape

Description:
A prioritized list of voice family names that contain specific voices

Value:
specific-voice
generic-voice

Type:
Aural

See also:
azimuth, cue, cue-after, cue-before, elevation, pause, pause-after, pause-before, pitch, pitch-range, play-during, richness, speak, speak-numeral, speak-punctuation, speech-rate, stress, volume

volume CSS 2.0

Browser Version:

IE	FireFox	Netscape

Description:
Specifies the volume of the speaking

Value:
number
%
silent
x-soft
soft
medium
loud
x-loud

Type:
Aural

See also:
azimuth, cue, cue-after, cue-before, elevation, pause, pause-after, pause-before, pitch, pitch-range, play-during, richness, speak, speak-numeral, speak-punctuation, speech-rate, stress, voice-family

white-space CSS 1.0

Browser Version:

IE	FireFox	Netscape
5	1	4

Description:
Sets how white space inside an element is handled

Value:
normal
pre
nowrap

Type:
Text

See also:
letter-spacing, text-align, text-align-last, text-decoration, text-indent, text-shadow, text-transform, text-underline-position, word-spacing, word-wrap

widows CSS 2.0

Browser Version:

IE	FireFox	Netscape

Description:
Sets the minimum number of lines for a paragraph that must be left at the top of a page

Value:
number

Type:
Printing

See also:
marks, orphans, page, page-break-after, page-break-before, page-break-inside, size

width CSS 1.0

Browser Version:

IE	FireFox	Netscape
4	1	4

Description:
Sets the width of an element

Value:
auto
%
length

Type:
Dimensions

See also:
height, line-height, max-height, max-width, min-height, min-width

word-break CSS 2.0

Browser Version:

IE	FireFox	Netscape
5.0	-	-

Description:
This property controls the line breaking behavior within words.

Value:
break-all
keep-all
normal

Type:
International

See also:
direction, ime-mode, layout-flow, layout-grid, layout-grid-char, layout-grid-char-spacing, layout-grid-line, layout-grid-type, line-break, ruby-align, ruby-overhang, ruby-position, text-autospace, text-justify, text-kashida-space, unicode-bidi, writing-mode

word-spacing CSS 1.0

Browser Version:

IE	FireFox	Netscape
6	1	6

Description:
Increase or decrease the space between words

Value:
normal
length

Type:
Text

See also:
letter-spacing, text-align, text-align-last, text-decoration, text-indent, text-shadow, text-transform, text-underline-position, white-space, word-wrap

word-wrap CSS 2.0

Browser Version:

IE	FireFox	Netscape
5.5	-	-

Description:
Specifies whether the current rendered line should break if the content exceeds the boundary of the specified rendering box for an element

Value:
break-word
normal

Type:
Text

See also:
letter-spacing, text-align, text-align-last, text-decoration, text-indent, text-shadow, text-transform, text-underline-position, white-space, word-spacing

writing-mode CSS 2.0

Browser Version:

IE	FireFox	Netscape
5.5	-	-

Description:
This property controls the intrinsic writing direction rendering for a block of content.

Value:
lr-tb
tb-rl

Type:
International

See also:
direction, ime-mode, layout-flow, layout-grid, layout-grid-char, layout-grid-char-spacing, layout-grid-line, layout-grid-type, line-break, ruby-align, ruby-overhang, ruby-position, text-autospace, text-justify, text-kashida-space, unicode-bidi, word-break

z-index CSS 2.0

Browser Version:

IE	FireFox	Netscape
4	1	6

Description:
Sets the stack order of an element

Value:
auto
number

Type:
Positioning

See also:
bottom, clip, left, overflow, overflow-x, overflow-y, right, text-overflow, top, vertical-align

zoom CSS 2.0

Browser Version:

IE	FireFox	Netscape
5.5	-	-

Description:
This property controls the magnification level for the current element

Value:
normal
number
percentage

Type:
Dynamic Content

See also:
accelerator, behavior, cursor, filter

Appendixes

Appendix A: RGB Colors

Color Name	Color HEX
AliceBlue	#F0F8FF
AntiqueWhite	#FAEBD7
Aqua	#00FFFF
Aquamarine	#7FFFD4
Azure	#F0FFFF
Beige	#F5F5DC
Bisque	#FFE4C4
Black	#000000
BlanchedAlmond	#FFEBCD
Blue	#0000FF
BlueViolet	#8A2BE2
Brown	#A52A2A
BurlyWood	#DEB887
CadetBlue	#5F9EA0
Chartreuse	#7FFF00
Chocolate	#D2691E
Coral	#FF7F50
CornflowerBlue	#6495ED
Cornsilk	#FFF8DC
Crimson	#DC143C
Cyan	#00FFFF
DarkBlue	#00008B
DarkCyan	#008B8B
DarkGoldenRod	#B8860B
DarkGray	#A9A9A9
DarkGrey	#A9A9A9
DarkGreen	#006400
DarkKhaki	#BDB76B
DarkMagenta	#8B008B
DarkOliveGreen	#556B2F
Darkorange	#FF8C00
DarkOrchid	#9932CC
DarkRed	#8B0000
DarkSalmon	#E9967A
DarkSeaGreen	#8FBC8F

DarkSlateBlue	#483D8B
DarkSlateGray	#2F4F4F
DarkSlateGrey	#2F4F4F
DarkTurquoise	#00CED1
DarkViolet	#9400D3
DeepPink	#FF1493
DeepSkyBlue	#00BFFF
DimGray	#696969
DimGrey	#696969
DodgerBlue	#1E90FF
FireBrick	#B22222
FloralWhite	#FFFAF0
ForestGreen	#228B22
Fuchsia	#FF00FF
Gainsboro	#DCDCDC
GhostWhite	#F8F8FF
Gold	#FFD700
GoldenRod	#DAA520
Gray	#808080
Grey	#808080
Green	#008000
GreenYellow	#ADFF2F
HoneyDew	#F0FFF0
HotPink	#FF69B4
IndianRed	#CD5C5C
Indigo	#4B0082
Ivory	#FFFFF0
Khaki	#F0E68C
Lavender	#E6E6FA
LavenderBlush	#FFF0F5
LawnGreen	#7CFC00
LemonChiffon	#FFFACD
LightBlue	#ADD8E6
LightCoral	#F08080
LightCyan	#E0FFFF
LightGoldenRodYellow	#FAFAD2

LightGray	#D3D3D3
LightGrey	#D3D3D3
LightGreen	#90EE90
LightPink	#FFB6C1
LightSalmon	#FFA07A
LightSeaGreen	#20B2AA
LightSkyBlue	#87CEFA
LightSlateGray	#778899
LightSlateGrey	#778899
LightSteelBlue	#B0C4DE
LightYellow	#FFFFE0
Lime	#00FF00
LimeGreen	#32CD32
Linen	#FAF0E6
Magenta	#FF00FF
Maroon	#800000
MediumAquaMarine	#66CDAA
MediumBlue	#0000CD
MediumOrchid	#BA55D3
MediumPurple	#9370D8
MediumSeaGreen	#3CB371
MediumSlateBlue	#7B68EE
MediumSpringGreen	#00FA9A
MediumTurquoise	#48D1CC
MediumVioletRed	#C71585
MidnightBlue	#191970
MintCream	#F5FFFA
MistyRose	#FFE4E1
Moccasin	#FFE4B5
NavajoWhite	#FFDEAD
Navy	#000080
OldLace	#FDF5E6
Olive	#808000
OliveDrab	#6B8E23
Orange	#FFA500
OrangeRed	#FF4500

Orchid	#DA70D6
PaleGoldenRod	#EEE8AA
PaleGreen	#98FB98
PaleTurquoise	#AFEEEE
PaleVioletRed	#D87093
PapayaWhip	#FFEFD5
PeachPuff	#FFDAB9
Peru	#CD853F
Pink	#FFC0CB
Plum	#DDA0DD
PowderBlue	#B0E0E6
Purple	#800080
Red	#FF0000
RosyBrown	#BC8F8F
RoyalBlue	#4169E1
SaddleBrown	#8B4513
Salmon	#FA8072
SandyBrown	#F4A460
SeaGreen	#2E8B57
SeaShell	#FFF5EE
Sienna	#A0522D
Silver	#C0C0C0
SkyBlue	#87CEEB
SlateBlue	#6A5ACD
SlateGray	#708090
SlateGrey	#708090
Snow	#FFFAFA
SpringGreen	#00FF7F
SteelBlue	#4682B4
Tan	#D2B48C
Teal	#008080
Thistle	#D8BFD8
Tomato	#FF6347
Turquoise	#40E0D0
Violet	#EE82EE
Wheat	#F5DEB3

White	#FFFFFF
WhiteSmoke	#F5F5F5
Yellow	#FFFF00
YellowGreen	#9ACD32

Appendix B: ASCII Characters

Number	Character	Description
32		space
33	!	exclamation mark
34	"	quotation mark
35	#	number sign
36	$	dollar sign
37	%	percent sign
38	&	ampersand
39	'	apostrophe
40	(	left parenthesis
41	)	right parenthesis
42	*	asterisk
43	+	plus sign
44	,	comma
45	-	hyphen
46	.	period
47	/	slash
48	0	digit 0
49	1	digit 1
50	2	digit 2
51	3	digit 3
52	4	digit 4
53	5	digit 5
54	6	digit 6
55	7	digit 7
56	8	digit 8
57	9	digit 9
58	:	colon
59	;	semicolon
60	<	less-than
61	=	equals-to
62	>	greater-than
63	?	question mark
64	@	at sign
65	A	uppercase A
66	B	uppercase B
67	C	uppercase C

68	D	uppercase D
69	E	uppercase E
70	F	uppercase F
71	G	uppercase G
72	H	uppercase H
73	I	uppercase I
74	J	uppercase J
75	K	uppercase K
76	L	uppercase L
77	M	uppercase M
78	N	uppercase N
79	O	uppercase O
80	P	uppercase P
81	Q	uppercase Q
82	R	uppercase R
83	S	uppercase S
84	T	uppercase T
85	U	uppercase U
86	V	uppercase V
87	W	uppercase W
88	X	uppercase X
89	Y	uppercase Y
90	Z	uppercase Z
91	[	left square bracket
92	\	backslash
93	]	right square bracket
94	^	caret
95	_	underscore
96	`	grave accent
97	a	lowercase a
98	b	lowercase b
99	c	lowercase c
100	d	lowercase d
101	e	lowercase e
102	f	lowercase f
103	g	lowercase g
104	h	lowercase h

<table>
<tr><td>105</td><td>i</td><td>lowercase i</td></tr>
<tr><td>106</td><td>j</td><td>lowercase j</td></tr>
<tr><td>107</td><td>k</td><td>lowercase k</td></tr>
<tr><td>108</td><td>l</td><td>lowercase l</td></tr>
<tr><td>109</td><td>m</td><td>lowercase m</td></tr>
<tr><td>110</td><td>n</td><td>lowercase n</td></tr>
<tr><td>111</td><td>o</td><td>lowercase o</td></tr>
<tr><td>112</td><td>p</td><td>lowercase p</td></tr>
<tr><td>113</td><td>q</td><td>lowercase q</td></tr>
<tr><td>114</td><td>r</td><td>lowercase r</td></tr>
<tr><td>115</td><td>s</td><td>lowercase s</td></tr>
<tr><td>116</td><td>t</td><td>lowercase t</td></tr>
<tr><td>117</td><td>u</td><td>lowercase u</td></tr>
<tr><td>118</td><td>v</td><td>lowercase v</td></tr>
<tr><td>119</td><td>w</td><td>lowercase w</td></tr>
<tr><td>120</td><td>x</td><td>lowercase x</td></tr>
<tr><td>121</td><td>y</td><td>lowercase y</td></tr>
<tr><td>122</td><td>z</td><td>lowercase z</td></tr>
<tr><td>123</td><td>{</td><td>left curly brace</td></tr>
<tr><td>124</td><td>|</td><td>vertical bar</td></tr>
<tr><td>125</td><td>}</td><td>right curly brace</td></tr>
<tr><td>126</td><td>~</td><td>tilde</td></tr>
</table>

Appendix C: Latin-1 Character Entities

Result	Description	Entity Name	Entity Number
"	quotation mark	"	"
'	apostrophe	' (does not work in IE)	'
&	ampersand	&	&
<	less-than	<	<
>	greater-than	>	>

Appendix D: ISO 8859-1 Symbol Entities

Result	Description	Entity Name	Entity Number
	non-breaking space		
¡	inverted exclamation mark	¡	¡
¢	cent	¢	¢
£	pound	£	£
¤	currency	¤	¤
¥	yen	¥	¥
¦	broken vertical bar	¦	¦
§	section	§	§
¨	spacing diaeresis	¨	¨
©	copyright	©	©
ª	feminine ordinal indicator	ª	ª
«	angle quotation mark (left)	«	«
¬	negation	¬	¬
	soft hyphen		
®	registered trademark	®	®
¯	spacing macron	¯	¯
°	degree	°	°
±	plus-or-minus	±	±
^{2}	superscript 2	²	²
^{3}	superscript 3	³	³
´	spacing acute	´	´
µ	micro	µ	µ
¶	paragraph	¶	¶
·	middle dot	·	·
¸	spacing cedilla	¸	¸
^{1}	superscript 1	¹	¹
º	masculine ordinal indicator	º	º
»	angle quotation mark (right)	»	»
¼	fraction 1/4	¼	¼
½	fraction 1/2	½	½
¾	fraction 3/4	¾	¾
¿	inverted question mark	¿	¿
×	multiplication	×	×
÷	division	÷	÷

Appendix E: ISO 8859-1 Character Entities

Result	Description	Entity Name	Entity Number
À	capital a, grave accent	À	À
Á	capital a, acute accent	Á	Á
Â	capital a, circumflex accent	Â	Â
Ã	capital a, tilde	Ã	Ã
Ä	capital a, umlaut mark	Ä	Ä
Å	capital a, ring	Å	Å
Æ	capital ae	Æ	Æ
Ç	capital c, cedilla	Ç	Ç
È	capital e, grave accent	È	È
É	capital e, acute accent	É	É
Ê	capital e, circumflex accent	Ê	Ê
Ë	capital e, umlaut mark	Ë	Ë
Ì	capital i, grave accent	Ì	Ì
Í	capital i, acute accent	Í	Í
Î	capital i, circumflex accent	Î	Î
Ï	capital i, umlaut mark	Ï	Ï
Ð	capital eth, Icelandic	Ð	Ð
Ñ	capital n, tilde	Ñ	Ñ
Ò	capital o, grave accent	Ò	Ò
Ó	capital o, acute accent	Ó	Ó
Ô	capital o, circumflex accent	Ô	Ô
Õ	capital o, tilde	Õ	Õ
Ö	capital o, umlaut mark	Ö	Ö
Ø	capital o, slash	Ø	Ø
Ù	capital u, grave accent	Ù	Ù
Ú	capital u, acute accent	Ú	Ú
Û	capital u, circumflex accent	Û	Û
Ü	capital u, umlaut mark	Ü	Ü
Ý	capital y, acute accent	Ý	Ý
Þ	capital THORN, Icelandic	Þ	Þ
ß	small sharp s, German	ß	ß
à	small a, grave accent	à	à
á	small a, acute accent	á	á
â	small a, circumflex accent	â	â
ã	small a, tilde	ã	ã
ä	small a, umlaut mark	ä	ä

å	small a, ring	å	å
æ	small ae	æ	æ
ç	small c, cedilla	ç	ç
è	small e, grave accent	è	è
é	small e, acute accent	é	é
ê	small e, circumflex accent	ê	ê
ë	small e, umlaut mark	ë	ë
ì	small i, grave accent	ì	ì
í	small i, acute accent	í	í
î	small i, circumflex accent	î	î
ï	small i, umlaut mark	ï	ï
ð	small eth, Icelandic	ð	ð
ñ	small n, tilde	ñ	ñ
ò	small o, grave accent	ò	ò
ó	small o, acute accent	ó	ó
ô	small o, circumflex accent	ô	ô
õ	small o, tilde	õ	õ
ö	small o, umlaut mark	ö	ö
ø	small o, slash	ø	ø
ù	small u, grave accent	ù	ù
ú	small u, acute accent	ú	ú
û	small u, circumflex accent	û	û
ü	small u, umlaut mark	ü	ü
ý	small y, acute accent	ý	ý
þ	small thorn, Icelandic	þ	þ
ÿ	small y, umlaut mark	ÿ	ÿ

Index

C

E

F

H

I

L

M

N

P

Q

R

S

T

www.ingramcontent.com/pod-product-compliance
Lightning Source LLC
Chambersburg PA
CBHW080142060326
40689CB00018B/3814

* 9 7 8 0 9 8 1 8 4 0 2 7 7 *